THE
Sock
KNITTING
BIBLE

THE Sock KNITTING BIBLE

Everything you need to know
about how to knit socks

LYNNE ROWE

DAVID & CHARLES

www.davidandcharles.com

CONTENTS

Introduction **6**

How to use this book **8**

All about socks 10
Sock anatomy 12
Measuring foot size 14
Choosing the correct size 15

Tools and materials 16
Yarn 18
Hand-dyed vs machine-dyed 18
Yarn colours 18
How to knit matching socks 22
Yarn fibres 24
Yarn weight/thickness 25

Needles 26
Needle materials 26
Needle types 26

Extras 28

Checking your tension/gauge 30
Importance of tension/gauge 32
Substituting yarn 32
Swatching 34
Measuring your tension/gauge 36
Achieving tension/gauge in a pattern 37

Sock recipes 38
Getting started 40
Cuff-down socks 42
Toe-up socks 50
Two-needle socks 58
Variations on the sock recipes 66
Contrast cuffs, heels and toes 66
Scrappy socks 68
Shortie socks 68
No-heel socks 68

Sock elements 70
Cuffs 72
1 x 1 rib cuff 74
2 x 2 rib cuff 74
3 x 1 rib cuff 74
Half-twisted rib cuff 75
Two-colour rib cuff (corrugated rib cuff) 75
Picot edge cuff 75

Heels 76
Cuff-down heel flap and gusset options 78
Common heel (stocking (stockinette) stitch with garter stitch edge) 78
Slipstitch heel 80
Garter stitch heel 80
Striped (two-colour) heel 81
Toe-up options 82
Simple shaped heel 82
Double stitch short row heel (boomerang heel) 82
Wrap and turn short row heel 83
Toe-up gusset and heel flap 84
Forethought heel 85

Toes 86
Toes for cuff-down socks 88
Classic wedge toe 88
Rounded toe 88
Four-point toe 89
Toes for toe-up socks 89
Basic toe 89
Banded toe 89

Sock projects 90
Sloping Hills by Winwick Mum 92
Under the Stars by Emma Potter 96
Twisting Pathways by Vikki Bird 100
Spring Lace by Rachel Fletcher 104
Bracken Cables by Olivia Villareal 108
Summer Meadows by Carmen Jorissen 112
Autumn Berries by Kaitlin Barthold 116
Red Sky At Night by Abby Brown 120
Beads of Dew by Anniken Allis 124
Winter Snow by Kerstin Balke 128

Knitting in the round 132

On double-pointed needles (DPNs) 134

Joining the round 135

On a short circular needle 136

On a long circular needle for magic loop 137

On flexible short needles 138

Two at a time magic loop knitting 140

Sock techniques 144

Casting on 146
Long-tail cast on (thumb method) 146
German twisted cast on 146
Cable cast on (two-needle cast on) 147
Alternating cable cast on 147
Judy's magic cast on 148

Basic stitches 149
Knit stitch 149
Purl stitch 149
Slip stitch 150
K1tbl (knit 1 through the back leg) 150

Reading charts 150

Increasing 151
Kfb (knit front and back) 151
Yarn over increases (yo) 151
Make 1 stitch (M1L & M1R) 151

Decreasing 152
Right-leaning decreases (k2tog, p2tog) 152
Left-leaning decreases (skpo, ssk) 152
Double decreases (cdd, k3tog, sk2po) 152

Adding beads 153

Picking up stitches 154
Along edge from right side of work 154
Along edge from wrong side of work 154
From waste yarn for forethought heel 154

Cables 155

Short rows 156
Wrap and turn (W&T) short rows 156
Double stitch short rows (German short rows) 157

Working with more than one yarn/colour 158
Holding two yarns together at once 158
Changing colours 158
Carrying yarn along inside of your work 159
Jogless stripes 159
Corrugated rib 160
Stranded colourwork and Fair Isle knitting 160

Casting (binding) off 161
Knit cast (bind) off (in the round) 161
Knit cast (bind) off (working flat) 161
Three-needle cast (bind) off 161
Jeny's surprisingly stretchy cast (bind) off 162

Finishing your project 163
Grafting/Kitchener stitch 163
Mattress stitch 163
Weaving in ends 164
Fixing holes 164
Blocking your project 165

Abbreviations 166

About the author 166

Index 167

Thanks 168

The designers 168

Introduction

If I could only knit one type of project for the rest of my knitting days, I would definitely choose socks. There are so many variations and so many techniques to discover and learn that I could happily sit with my sock yarn and needles and knit these amazing tubular structures for ever, creating something different every time.

I love the never-ending possibilities of all the combinations. There are long socks, short socks, ankle socks, plain socks, striped socks or patterned socks, and it doesn't matter how many pairs I knit as I know they will always come in handy and, as well as being practical, there's definitely something magical and mindful about knitting socks. You can patiently sit, working stitch by stitch, round by round and before you know it, you're in your calm zone feeling relaxed and peaceful and another sock is flying off the needles.

I'm delighted to share all my skills and knowledge with you in the form of this reference bible, which I've written with both new and experienced sock knitters in mind. I've covered all aspects of sock knitting, from beginner's basics, through to more advanced techniques, so that you can choose to keep it really simple or 'step it up' and go for a more intricate combination of stitch patterns and techniques.

My handy guide to all the different sock yarns will help you choose the right yarns for your hand-knitted socks, and the illustrated guides on how to knit in the round will help you knit with any sort of knitting needles. I've even included recipes for a two-needle sock and a sock with no heel, either of which could be a great way to start your sock knitting journey.

There are so many things to try and new skills to learn, which is really exciting and is sure to 'keep you on your toes'.

I've split the book into sections so that you can tackle things step-by-step and work at your own pace, without feeling overwhelmed.

- The first section covers all the different parts of a sock and how to measure your feet to work out how long and wide to knit your socks.

- In the second section we look at the the essential materials that you will need, with an in-depth guide to yarn and needles, through to optional extras such as row counters, project bags and blocking equipment.

- The third section addresses every aspect of tension/gauge to help you knit socks that fit.

- Then we move on to the fourth section which takes you through the basic patterns for each type of sock, including toe-up, cuff-down, two-needle and no-heel socks.

- The fifth section provides a variety of cuffs, heels and toes, so that you have all the tools at hand to mix and match these elements in your knitted socks.

- In the sixth section I feature 10 amazing sock designers, each sharing an exclusive pattern for you to try, with a mix of beautiful textures, cables, lace and colourwork. You're sure to find something that's just up your street.

- The final sections contain all the knitting techniques that you need to knit socks, including how to knit in the round with different needles, jogless stripes, adding beads, colourwork, two-at-a-time sock knitting, plus lots more.

So everything is here for you to start, or continue, your sock knitting adventures.

Whichever projects you choose, I hope this sock bible will be a useful resource for years to come, as you build up your own colourful and cosy hand-knitted sock drawer.

Happy sock knitting,

How to use this book

If you're completely new to sock knitting, then this book is a great place to start. If you follow the steps below, they will take you through all the aspects of knitting a sock, from exploring the parts of the sock itself, through to choosing yarn and needles ready for casting on.

If you've already knitted socks there are many different sock elements that you could try in **Sock elements: Cuffs**, **Heels** and **Toes**, and lots of gorgeous socks to knit in the **Sock projects** section, where our featured designers showcase different knitting techniques, such as cables, lace, colourwork and using beads.

And don't worry if ultimately you still prefer to knit flat, because we have included a two-needle sock recipe, so there is something for everyone.

Here are the steps to follow before you start knitting your socks:

1. Read the **Sock anatomy** section in **All about socks**, to explore all the different sock elements you will be knitting.

2. Follow the guidance in **Measuring foot size** to determine the length and circumference of your feet so that you know the measurements you are knitting to (when I say 'your feet' or 'your foot' throughout the book I mean the foot of the person who will ultimately be wearing your socks).

3. Read through all the **Tools and materials** section to help you choose the most suitable needles and yarn.

4. For your chosen needles, practise casting on, knitting in the round on a small swatch and casting (binding) off as explained in **Knitting in the round** and **Sock techniques**.

5. Read through **Checking your tension/gauge** and use your swatch to check your stitches are the right size so that your socks will fit.

6. Use your tension/gauge and foot measurements to work out which size sock to knit.

7. If needed, refresh your general knitting techniques as illustrated in **Sock techniques**.

8. Choose your preferred socks and variations from **Sock recipes**, and you're ready to cast on!

Once you have mastered the basics you can move on to **Sock projects** and try all the different socks by our featured designers.

And if at any point you get stuck, just flick through the book and use it as a reference point.

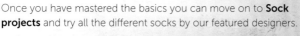

ALL ABOUT SOCKS

There are lots of different parts to a hand-knitted sock and this bible provides many different techniques for the same element, so that you have a nice selection of choices to mix and match and make your socks more personal and unique.

You can see all the different parts of a sock in the annotated sample (see Sock anatomy), where I've used different colours of yarn for the different features so they are easier to identify. As you begin knitting your sock, you will see that some elements are really simple and others are a little more complex.

The main thing to remember is that the basic parts of a sock remain unchanged from sock to sock and, as the knitter, you can decide for yourself which methods and techniques you prefer to use, such as the way you cast on or the way that you pick up stitches.

SOCK ANATOMY

Cuff

The cuff is the very top of the sock and, as well as being decorative, it has the really important function of holding up your sock by gripping around your calf, leg or ankle. The cuff therefore usually needs to be a stretchy fabric that will spring back into shape, often knitted with alternating knit and purl stitches as ribbing. The specific type of rib can vary from pattern to pattern, but cuffs shouldn't be too loose nor too tight (see Sock elements: Cuffs).

Leg

The leg of a sock sits below the cuff and above the heel, and it can vary dramatically in length – from over-the-knee stockings, down to ankle length socks, while some trainer (sneaker) socks miss out the leg completely, moving straight from the cuff to the heel. You can have plain legs, patterned legs, stripy legs, lacy legs or textured legs. There are so many variations that I'm sure you could knit socks forever and never use the same pattern twice.

Heel

Almost all socks have a heel (the only exception being a no-heel tube sock). A sock heel is a small pocket of knitting that will allow the sock to fit snuggly around your foot's heel. There are lots of different ways to knit heels and these will depend on whether you start your knitting at the toe, or at the cuff. They're great fun to try and you may find that some heels will feel more comfortable than others (see Sock elements: Heels).

Foot

The foot of a sock extends from the end of the heel section, to the start of the toe section, with a top (instep) and bottom (sole and arch). You can adjust the sock foot length to your foot, and this is often explained in a sock pattern (see Choosing the correct size).

Instep

The instep of your foot is the curved top of your foot from your ankle to your toes. The instep of the sock may continue the pattern from the leg or be plain to fit better inside your shoe.

Gusset

The gusset on a sock is created at the point where your foot is likely to be largest in circumference. Many socks have additional stitches on the needles at this point to accommodate this extra width. Thus the gusset may be shaped, either by increasing or decreasing, depending on whether you're knitting cuff-down or toe-up socks.

Sole

The underside or bottom of a sock is the sole and usually this will be in stocking (stockinette) stitch, rather than a more elaborate stitch pattern, so that it is really smooth and comfortable. It's the part of the sock that takes the most impact and is the part of our foot that is likely to sweat most.

Arch

The arch is at the centre of the underside of your foot between the toe and heel on the sole, and is opposite to the instep. Some sock designs add a ribbed arch to help keep the sock in place and to also add a bit of arch support.

Toe

A sock toe is usually shaped by increasing or decreasing to create a snug place for your toes. The method will depend on whether the sock toes are knitted first or last. Some sock toes are worked in exactly the same way as a heel, following the same technique. You may find that some sock toe shapes will feel more comfortable than others to wear, so do be sure to try different ones (see Sock elements: Toes).

Toe seam

Whether you start or end at the toe of the sock, the toe seam will often be designed for comfort and to avoid abrasion. There are many ways to close a toe, and some methods create a more blended finish than others. When working cuff-down, Kitchener stitch is a popular choice because it leaves a smooth join (see Sock techniques: Finishing your project).

Cuff

Leg

Instep

Foot

Heel

Gusset

Arch

Sole

Toe seam

Toe

MEASURING FOOT SIZE

Before you begin knitting your socks, you will need to first measure your foot so that you knit to the correct size. To do this, follow the instructions below and make a note of your measurements and keep them somewhere safe for future reference. I'd recommend drawing (tracing) all around your foot too, so that you can create a template to cut out and keep.

Your foot template will come in really handy when a pattern tells you to knit the foot of your sock until it measures a given amount of less than the full length. Instead of trying to work this out on your foot, you can use your template instead.

Foot length

1. Take a piece of paper large enough to accommodate your whole foot and place it on a hard, flat surface.

2. With your foot on the paper, use a pen or pencil to mark the back of the heel and the tip of the longest toe.

3. Using a straight ruler, measure the distance between the 2 points. This is your foot length.

If desired, draw (trace) around your foot and cut out your foot template to use as a guide for heel and toe placement later.

Foot circumference

1. Take a soft tape measure and place it around the widest part of your foot. Don't pull the tape measure too tightly, but don't leave it too loose either. This is your foot circumference.

Make sure that you measure both feet as they may not be identical. Use the larger measurement if they differ.

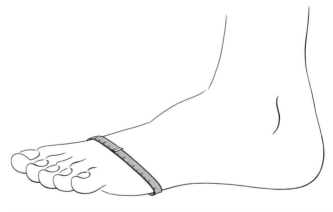

CHOOSING THE CORRECT SIZE

Negative ease

You may encounter the phrase 'negative ease', which is often used in knitting patterns. Negative ease means that your final knitted piece is **smaller** than your actual measurements, but there is enough stretch within the knitted fabric to allow the piece to fit and move comfortably.

For socks, this means that your completed sock should be smaller than the measured circumference of your foot, so that it stretches slightly when worn to ensure a comfortable and snug fit.

The big question here is how much smaller do you knit?

As a guide, I would suggest that **5% negative ease** is adequate for a sock, therefore you should knit to 5% smaller than your actual foot circumference.

To work this out, use the following formula:

A - B = C

Where:

A = your foot circumference (in centimetres or inches)

B = 5% of your foot circumference; you can work this out by multiplying your 'A' number by 0.05

C = the result of (A) minus (B)

To use my foot circumference as an example:

A = 20cm (8in)

B = 1cm (⅜in); 20cm (8in) multiplied by 0.05 = 1cm (⅜in)

C = 20cm (8in) minus 1cm (⅜in) = 19cm (7⅝in)

Therefore a sock to fit my 20cm (8in) foot circumference should be knitted to 19cm (7⅝in) circumference.

If you prefer a tighter fitting sock, you could apply a greater negative ease to your foot circumference. For example, if you want **10% negative ease**, then work out B by multiplying your 'A' number by 0.10 instead of 0.05, then subtracting this figure to determine C.

For a looser fitting sock, such as a bed sock, you may prefer to apply **no ease**, so you would then knit to the exact measurement of your foot circumference. In this case, A equals C, so just knit to the same measurement as your foot.

Whether or not you also apply negative ease to the foot length is entirely a personal choice. My preference is to work socks to the same length as the actual foot length and not apply additional negative ease, otherwise they may feel constricting on your toes.

Remember that you can knit your foot length to any shoe size (foot length) regardless of how many stitches you cast on. If you're knitting for yourself, you can easily measure the length of your own foot using paper and a pencil as I've described, but if you are knitting socks to gift, you may need to knit to a given foot size for length, and these are provided for guidance in the table below.

UK size	Euro size	US women's size	US men's size	Total foot length (cm)	Total foot length (in)
2	35	4	2.5	21	8¼
3	36	5	3.5	22	8½
4	37	6	4.5	22.5	8¾
5	38	7	5.5	23.5	9¼
6	39	8	6.5	24	9½
7	40	9	7.5	25	9¾
8	41	10	8.5	26	10¼
9	42	11	9.5	26.5	10½
10	43	12	10.5	27	10¾
11	44	13	11.5	28	11
12	45	14	12.5	28.5	11¼

Now that you know how long and wide to knit your socks, you will need to know your knitting tension/gauge in order to work out the number of stitches you need to cast on or which size sock you would knit from the pattern so that your socks are the perfect fit and don't end up too baggy or too tight. This is covered in detail later (see Checking your tension/gauge).

TOOLS AND MATERIALS

The great thing about sock knitting is that you don't need a lot of different materials. With just yarn, needles and a tape measure you're ready to go, but like any craft hobby, there are so many options and products available, and many different price points. This means that you really do have a huge range of yarns and needle types to choose from, so I've written a handy guide to help you navigate through the different products available.

Yarn

You can buy almost any yarn fibre for socks, from wool (with or without nylon), through to bamboo, silk, cotton and cashmere blends. Different types of yarn will produce different results, so depending on what you want to achieve, and the type of sock you want to wear, you will need to make sure that you choose the right yarn for your needs.

And in addition, regardless of the fibre content, you can buy yarns that are either single-coloured or multi-coloured, including variegated, speckled, self-patterning and self-striping yarns. These multi-coloured yarns are vast and varied and can create an abundance of socks that are all completely different in appearance, so it will all come down to a personal preference as to the yarn you choose for your socks.

I have provided some in-depth guidance below to help you find your preferred yarns, firstly talking about colours and dyes, followed by the fibre content and thickness.

If you're not sure of how your yarn will look when knitted up with a specific stitch pattern, it's definitely worth knitting up a small sample to get a good idea of the finished appearance (see Checking your tension/gauge: Swatching). Your yarn may look quite different if you are knitting lace compared to knitting cables or a more textured knit/purl combination.

I hope you have great fun trying out different yarns for your sock projects.

Hand-dyed vs machine-dyed

Machine-dyed yarns are usually manufactured on a larger scale and will come with a ball band, shade code or name and a lot number (or a dye number), so that individual balls can be easily matched. Because they are painted by a machine, the spacing of the colours during the dye process can be more consistent and uniform, and therefore more easily repeatable for their large-scale production. Machine-dyed yarns can also be slightly harder wearing than a hand-dyed yarn, as the yarn itself is often slightly more robust and can also sometimes be machine washed. So machine-dyed yarns can offer great value for money.

Hand-dyed yarns on the other hand are painted independently, by skilled artisans whose canvas is the yarn base – most commonly the base is an un-dyed skein or hank of yarn. Yarn dyers apply their dyes creatively to the yarn base in different ways, in order to achieve stunning effects that are perfect for sock knitting. Because of the individuality of the skeins and the smaller-scale methods of production, it can be much harder to create dye lots that are completely identical, or colour patterns that match exactly. However, the great thing about sock knitting is that matching skeins is less of a problem because you will only need one single 100g (3.5oz) skein for most calf-length socks. So if you have lots of single skeins or balls of yarn in your stash, then sock knitting could be the perfect stash-busting solution.

Yarn colours

Knitters use yarn like artists use paint, so it's always worth taking time to consider the look you want for your socks. Note that lighter colours tend to show off some stitch patterns more clearly than others, so think ahead when you are pairing a design with a yarn. And of course it's always worth knitting up a small sample of the pattern before you begin with your chosen yarn to make sure you are getting the look you desire (see Checking your tension/gauge: Swatching).

SINGLE COLOURS (ALSO CALLED SOLID COLOURS)

Sometimes yarn that is a single colour is also called a solid colour because it is all the same colour throughout with no variation. Solid colours can be incredibly rich and vibrant and the colour itself can be the star of the sock show. Without using any fancy stitch patterns, you can create a beautiful, strong coloured sock, either by using the solid colour throughout or by adding a bold contrast colour for cuffs, heels and toes.

SEMI-SOLID COLOURS

These yarns are still one colour, but unlike a solid colour, they contain a range of lighter and darker shades or tones of the same colour (often called tonal colours). Sometimes these variations stand out more clearly because the differences between the lighter and darker shades are more notable.

SPECKLED YARNS

This is without doubt one of my favourite types of yarn, where small specks of colour are spattered onto either a plain or semi-solid background, creating a flecked or dotted appearance. I love how the little pops of colour create a visually striking and pretty pattern. Speckled yarns look amazing for socks, especially when they are combined with a solid and bold contrasting cuff, heel and toe.

VARIEGATED OR MULTI-COLOURED

A yarn that has lots of short colour changes can be called multi-coloured or variegated. These can be bold and bright, or muted and more gently contrasting. If you love colour, then a very busy variegated yarn with lots of bright colours may be perfect for your socks. On the other hand, you may find it overwhelming and distracting and it may hide a lovely stitch pattern. Sometimes the yarn may look really beautiful in the skein, but it can knit up completely differently, which is something to look out for.

POOLING

The main issue you can get with a variegated yarn is colour pooling, or puddling, which can create a challenge to sock knitting. The factors that cause unintentional colour pooling are many. It can depend on where you start knitting the yarn from the ball, on the number of stitches being used, or on the stitch pattern, tension/gauge or needle size you are working with. Just by pure chance, you can end up with the short strips of the same colour or shade positioned in the same place on subsequent rounds (rather than being distributed more randomly) and this will result in a notable splodge or puddle of the same colour. This can sometimes look unsightly and may cause a distraction from a pretty stitch pattern and spoil your socks.

If colour pooling happens most unexpectedly, you can try changing your tension/gauge. If you change your needle size (by using the next size up or down) then the colour pattern could spread out differently and this may help to stop the pooling. If not, you could try a different stitch pattern to avoid pooling. Some people embrace the random nature of pooling and the unique 'fraternal twin' pair of socks that result.

Variegated yarn can look quite busy when knitting into socks (as in the top pair), or may create unexpected colour pooling patterns, with both socks looking quite different to each other (as in the bottom pair).

SELF-STRIPING OR SELF-PATTERNING YARNS

These yarns are in a league of their own and it's quite magical that you can create the most amazing socks that add stripes or other patterns without any hard work at all. The available colour combinations and varieties are so vast and, even better, the colour matching has already been done for you.

The best part is that you don't need to physically change colours and won't have lots of yarn tails to weave in. You simply cast on and knit from a single ball or skein, and hey presto – before you know it you have a colourful and eye-catching pair of socks.

When using these yarns, the main issue to consider is how to maintain the continuity of stripes or patterning around the heel/gusset area. This is particularly important if you are knitting a standard heel flap and gusset. Working in rows with only half the number of stitches for the heel flap means any stripes or colourwork pattern will be twice as deep at this point and will look notably different to the rest of your sock. And when you pick up the stitches around the heel flap to work the gusset, you will have a lot more stitches and therefore the colour pattern/striping will change again. On the gusset, more stitches means that any stripes or colourwork pattern will be narrower for this section, until you have decreased back to the final number of stitches for the foot.

All of these changes in striping or colourwork pattern could result in a sock that isn't uniform throughout, potentially making the heel and gusset area look out of balance.

To avoid this, you can try an afterthought heel or a short row heel (see Sock elements: Heels), which minimizes the pattern disruption along the main leg of your sock.

How to knit matching socks

It's often a personal choice as to whether to knit a pair of socks that match exactly or not to worry too much about it and just to go with the flow of the yarn.

Here are a few handy tips to help you match up your socks if your yarn has a very distinct pattern.

Start using your yarn from the same part of the ball for both socks: either pull the yarn from the centre of your ball, thus working from the centre of the ball to the outside, or pull the yarn from the outside of your ball, thus working from the outside of the ball to the centre. Working in the same way for both socks will ensure that any stripe or patterning sequence is running in the same order and will create the same colour sequence.

In addition, make your initial slip knot at the same point along the yarn's pattern for each sock. Sometimes this means cutting off small sections of yarn in order to reach the correct starting point, but you can keep these oddments for scrappy socks or for other yarn scrap projects.

If it helps, take a photo or make a note of where in the yarn patterning you made your initial slip knot for your first sock, so that you can use it as a reference for where to begin your second sock.

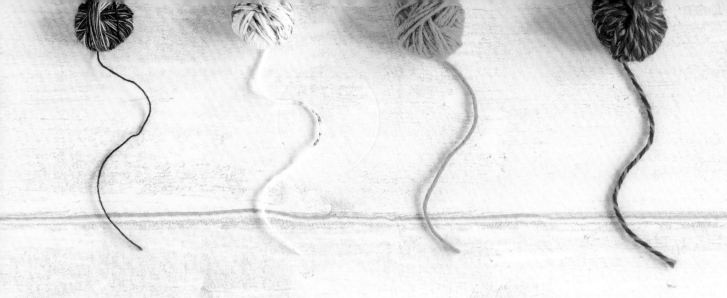

Yarn fibres

Yarn is made from all sorts of different fibres and these can be spun together in different ways to create varying strengths and thicknesses of yarn. This quick guide is a good starting point to help you choose from the wide choice that is available.

WOOL WITH NYLON OR POLYAMIDE

Wool is the main fibre recommended for everyday socks or walking socks, due to its insulating and wicking properties, and you'll find that the majority of yarn that is sold as 'sock yarn' contains wool with a small percentage of nylon or polyamide.

The fibre content is usually 75% wool or a wool blend, with 25% nylon (or polyamide), but you may see other combinations, such as 80% wool with 20% nylon. The manmade fibre element is combined with the wool to add elasticity and durability, so that your socks can be worn and washed over and over again.

The wool element can be a single type of wool such as Bluefaced Leicester or Merino, or it can be a blend of different wools. The main thing to look for is a tight twist, as this is likely to be harder wearing, rather than a single ply of yarn that is much softer and less durable. A softer, single-ply yarn is more likely to snap easily when you try to break it, whereas yarn with a tighter twist will need scissors to cut it.

Some sock yarns are labelled as 'superwash' and these have been treated to make them softer and machine washable. The process also helps the dye to absorb more deeply and therefore the colours of superwash yarn can be much more vibrant and colourful, as well as being more stable and less likely to bleed or run into other colours.

WOOL (NO NYLON)

With plastic microfibre pollution from synthetic fibres in our clothing becoming an increasingly serious issue, many knitters are now investigating the benefits and options available for using no-nylon wools for their hand knits.

While hand-knitted socks are only a very small fraction of this environmental problem due to the small amount of manmade fibre content (usually about 25% nylon or polyamide), nevertheless it is still a contributory factor and can raise concerns with knitters.

There has been a lot of research into no-nylon sock yarns, and you can find this widely on the internet by typing 'no nylon sock yarn' into your search bar. Here I'll also share a few helpful tips to help make your no-nylon woollen socks last a little bit longer.

- Try knitting with tough, strong wool that has a tighter twist and doesn't pill easily (rather than a single ply of yarn that snaps easily). Bluefaced Leicester with a tight twist might be a good starting point.

- You can knit with an extra strand of yarn at the pressure points (usually heels and toes) and also use a reinforcing stitch pattern at these areas, such as a slipstitch rib (commonly used with a standard heel flap). This could be a strand of the same yarn, or a strand of a different and stronger yarn, such as silk.

- Another pressure point on a sock can be the sole itself, so you could address this by adding rows of small running stitches across the sole to add a reinforcing layer and provide a bit of added strength.

- You could work an afterthought heel, and also knit it with 2 strands held together. This type of heel provides a better opportunity to remove and re-knit the heel should it wear through.

- There is even an option to knit the main sock with no-nylon wool then just use small skeins or oddments of wool with nylon to knit the heels and toes. This would at least reduce the amount of nylon being used overall.

OTHER NATURAL FIBRES

You may wonder if you can knit socks with non-wool yarns, such as bamboo, cotton or alpaca. The answer is that in reality you can knit a pair of socks from any yarn, but the deciding factor is what you are using them for and how fitted, loose, warm, strong they need to be.

For example, a pair of bed socks would only be used in the house without shoes or boots and thus not be subjected to the same abrasion that a pair of rugged outdoor walking socks would; the walking socks need yarn with good strength and durability, such as wool with reinforced heels, while the bed socks may be fine in alpaca or bamboo.

Some yarns made from plant fibres (bamboo, linen, cotton) may be durable but don't have the elasticity to pull over your heel to maintain a close fit. Yarns made from other animal fibres (alpaca, cashmere) may not be spun as tightly as wool and could look good but not last as well through regular wear.

There are a lot of options and blends with other fibres that you can try. When in doubt, see if the yarn is firstly marketed as a sock yarn, then also ask your knitter friends, carefully read reviews and/or request advice from your local knitting shop.

Yarn weight/thickness

As with yarn fibre, theoretically you can use any weight or thickness of yarn to knit socks, but the limiting factor will be whether you can still wear your shoes or boots over them. So the most common project options are regular 4ply sock yarns (also called fingering weight) which produce light, thin yet warm socks and allow a good number of stitches with which to make patterns with. You can also use thicker or heavier weight yarns, such as sport weight (5ply) or a 6ply yarn, or even double knitting (DK or 8ply). If you use anything thicker than DK (including aran/worsted, chunky or bulky), you would be unlikely to wear these with shoes, but they could make bed socks for cosy nights.

Needles

Socks are usually knitted in the round, in a tube with no seaming, using your choice of needles; you can work in the round with a set of double-pointed needles (also known as DPNs), a short circular needle, a long circular needle or a set of flexible short needles. You can even knit a sock flat using 2 straight knitting needles (see Sock recipes: Two-needle socks). Full tutorials on how to cast on and knit with these different needle types are provided in Knitting in the round.

In addition, each of these needle types can be made from a variety of materials: plastic, wood, metal or carbon fibre.

We will look at these different materials first.

Needle materials

Plastic needles are lightweight and flexible, and are warm to hold, but they can also warp or break easily. You may find that your yarn squeaks against the plastic which can be annoying, but they are an affordable choice, and many sock knitters love them.

Wooden needles offer lots of choice, from ebony or rosewood, to bamboo or birch, and are also warm to hold. The more you use them, the more your stitches will slide easily across them; however, like plastic needles, they can bend or warp and sometimes snap. They tend to be more expensive, ranging in price depending on the wood used; bamboo needles are usually the cheaper option.

Metal needles are widely available and very popular because they are both affordable and less prone to warping or breaking. They can last for years and years and are often passed down from generation to generation. However, they can be cold to the touch and therefore cause some pain and discomfort, especially if you suffer with arthritis. In addition, they can be quite slippery which means that your stitches can easily fall off the needles (especially the ends of DPNs).

Carbon fibre needles are a relatively new development and are becoming a firm favourite for many knitters. They are much less slippery than metal and they are stronger than plastic or wood. Usually they have metal tips to aid smooth and fast knitting. However, they are quite expensive so it would be worth trying a pair first before buying a full set, just in case you don't enjoy knitting with them.

Needle types

For the different types of needles for knitting in the round, a step-by-step guide for casting on and using each is included in Knitting in the round, with a short summary also included here.

DPNs (double-pointed needles): These are pointed at both ends so that you can access the stitches from either end of a needle and knit in the round. They come in sets of 4, 5 or 6 needles, and generally vary in length from around 10cm (4in) to 25cm (10in), or longer for specialist non-sock knitters.

A short circular needle: These are specifically designed with sock knitting in mind and are 2 small needle tips that are connected by a shorter, flexible cable, usually about 25cm (10in) long and designed to be shorter than the circumference of the sock so that you can bring the needle tips together to knit. The stitches flow around the needle from round to round really easily and seamlessly. Some short circular needles have one needle tip longer than the other and you would hold the longer tip for a more comfortable feel and knit with the shorter tip. But because the needle tips can be quite short in length, some knitters find these uncomfortable to knit with.

A long circular needle: You can use a long circular needle for sock knitting (the same type of long circular needle that you would knit a cowl or jumper on) by a method referred to as 'magic loop'. It's a great technique to use if you want to avoid buying extra needles, or if you find knitting with DPNs too tricky.

A set of flexible short needles: These are made from metal with a short flexible wire at the centre. They are almost a hybrid of other options and you use them in a similar way to the magic loop method, splitting the total number of stitches over 2 of the needles and working with the third.

Straight knitting needles: These are regular knitting needles that come in pairs and have a stopper at one end to prevent your stitches falling off. Straight needles are used to knit back and forth in rows, and come in different lengths to accommodate different numbers of stitches.

Note: The needle size depends on your knitting tension/gauge. Usually 2.5mm (US2 or US1) is recommended when working with sock yarn (4ply/fingering), but you may need a larger or smaller size to achieve the tension/gauge given in your chosen pattern, so you will need to check before you knit your first sock (see Checking your tension/gauge).

Extras

A hard, see-through ruler: for measuring tension/gauge.

Flexible tape measure: for measuring the length of your knitting and your foot measurements.

Row counter: helpful to keep a note of how many rows you've knitted.

Notebook and pen: to make notes of tension/gauge or any alterations you make to a pattern, and/or as an alternative to a row counter.

Project bag: perfect for keeping your work and equipment in.

Stitch markers: to mark the round or pattern repeats. Removable/hinged stitch markers are useful to place into stitches and ring stitch markers are useful to place on the needles, between stitches. You can also use short lengths of scrap yarn instead.

Stitch holders or waste yarn: for holding stitches. Make sure to use waste yarn that is thinner than your knitting yarn in a contrasting colour and a smooth fibre like cotton.

Cable needles: for temporarily holding stitches for quick access, such as for cables.

Crochet hook: for adding beads, if your pattern calls for them. Make sure the head of the crochet hook can fit easily through the hole in the bead.

Sharp scissors: for cutting the yarn.

Tapestry/yarn needle: a blunt ended wider needle for sewing and weaving in ends (a pointy needle will split your yarn and spoil your knitting).

Towel: for absorbing water when blocking your socks.

Wool wash: for soaking your socks (you can use a mild shampoo as an alternative).

Sock blockers: for blocking your socks (you can pin flat to dry as an alternative).

Yarn holder or yarn bowl: to hold a single ball of yarn while you knit, so that your yarn doesn't roll away (optional).

Yarn swift: for helping to wind off a skein of yarn (optional). You can also use your hands.

Yarn ball winder: for winding your skein of yarn into a yarn cake or ball (optional). You can also use your hands.

CHECKING YOUR TENSION/GAUGE

Every sock knitter does not have the same tension/gauge, even when knitting with the same yarn and needle size. There are many factors that affect tension/gauge, so it's important to check yours before you begin a project. Measuring with the yarn and needles for your chosen project will make sure that your knitting time isn't wasted by your socks not being the correct size for your feet.

IMPORTANCE OF TENSION/GAUGE

Checking the size of your knitted stitches before you begin your sock knitting is essential. You will first need to knit up a small amount of knitting (called a swatch or a tension/gauge square), and from it you can work out the size of your knitted stitches and rows.

For regular knitting, you would usually check your tension/gauge by knitting a small square, working in rows on 2 straight needles. This is the method you will use for your two-needle socks that are knitted flat.

But for sock knitting in the round, your knitted swatch will need to mirror the circular knitting of your socks and should not therefore be knitted flat in rows. Knitting in rows is not the same as knitting in the round, because when you work stocking (stockinette) stitch in the round, only knit stitches are used, whereas when you work stocking (stockinette) stitch flat in rows, both knit and purl stitches are used. Alternating between stitch types will affect your knitting tension/gauge; also knit and purl stitches are slightly different in size and therefore use slightly different amounts of yarn. So, for best results, you should knit your swatch in the round.

There are two ways of achieving this – you can knit in the round as if you are knitting a sock, or you can knit a flat swatch that mimics knitting in the round. Options for both methods are provided (see Swatching).

SUBSTITUTING YARN

Most sock patterns will suggest a specific yarn for a design, usually the yarn that has been used to knit up the designs, but this doesn't mean that you have to use the same yarn. There may be various reasons why you will want to use a different yarn; it could be that the yarn is no longer available, or you may simply prefer to use up yarn from your stash or something that suits your own needs or budget.

Here are a few tips to help you substitute yarn:

1. Fibre: Yarn fibres behave differently when knitted due to their characteristics, so it's important to substitute yarn that has a similar fibre content. For example if the original yarn is 100% Bluefaced Leicester wool, then you should try to find yarn with 100% wool content, or if the original yarn is 75% wool and 25% nylon, then you should try to use a similar combination of fibres.

2. Yarn thickness/weight: Choose the same yarn thickness/weight. For example if the pattern suggests a 4ply (fingering) weight yarn, then this would be your starting point to finding a suitable alternative.

3. Meterage/yardage of a skein/ball: This is always a good indication of yarn thickness as this can vary from one type of yarn to another, even for yarn of the same thickness/weight. If you look on the ball band you will see information about the yarn itself, including the length of yarn per skein/ball. For example, if the original yarn is 400m (438 yards) per 100g (3.5oz), then try to find a yarn that has the same meterage/yardage because if there are more (or less) metres/yards per 100g (3.5oz) then the yarn could be lighter/thinner (or heavier/thicker), which will affect your tension.

4. Tension/gauge: This is critical in yarn substitution. When you think you've found a suitable alternative based on the previous criteria, the next thing to do is to swatch (see Swatching). Only by swatching and checking your tension/gauge will you truly know whether your chosen yarn is a good substitute.

SWATCHING

Swatching in the round

This method is a great way to check your tension/gauge for plain, colourwork or patterned socks, or to see how your yarn will look when knitted in the round.

1. Cast on 64 stitches with 2.5mm (US2 or US1) needles, using the same type of needles that you will use to knit in the round (see Tools and materials: Needles).

2. Join to start knitting in the round (see Knitting in the round: Joining the round).

3. Purl a few rounds to create a neat edge then knit every round for approximately 10cm (4in).

4. Purl a few rounds to create another small edge, then cast off (see Sock techniques: Casting (binding) off).

You will have a knitted tube that looks like a wrist warmer (**a**).

5. It's a good idea to block your swatch (see Blocking your project in Sock Techniques: Finishing your project), pin it flat and leave it to dry completely. You can now measure the tension/gauge of your swatch (see Measuring your tension/gauge).

Swatching flat

There are 3 ways to create a flat swatch – cut a tube, work a stranded tension/gauge square, or work back and forth in rows. Once your flat swatch is complete, continue on to Measuring your tension/gauge.

CUT-OPEN TUBE

1. First knit a tube as for Swatching in the round, using 48 stitches in the round.

2. Before cutting, choose a line along which to cut the tube vertically, then first sew a back stitch along the length of the tube, on each side of your cutting line. This will prevent your stitches from unravelling. Alternatively you could use a crochet hook to add a crochet slip stitch along each side of your cutting line.

3. Next, cut between the sewn or crocheted stitches to open up your tube (**b**).

4. Pin the opened tube out, without stretching, and block it flat. Leave it to dry completely (**c**) before measuring your tension/gauge.

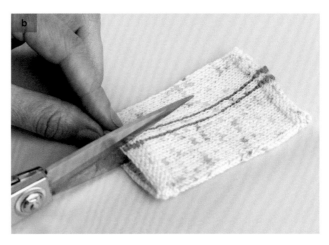

STRANDED TENSION/ GAUGE SQUARE

A stranded square is a flat piece of knitting that mimics working in the round, by only using knit stitches (**d**). In order to do this, yarn is stranded across the back of the knitting after each row, similar to knitting a very large i-cord (though you aren't pulling tight to form a tube) (**e**).

1. First, cast on approximately 45 stitches onto a 2.5mm (US2 or US1) DPN. Using a second DPN, work 4 rows flat in garter stitch (knit every row).

2. *Knit the next row but don't turn at the end, take the yarn loosely across the back of your work (similar to knitting an i-cord but don't pull it tightly). Repeat from * until your stocking (stockinette) stitch section measures approximately 11cm (4⅜in).

3. Work 4 rows flat in garter stitch and cast (bind) off.

4. Block your swatch and leave it to dry flat without stretching it before measuring your tension/gauge.

FLAT TENSION/GAUGE SQUARE

You will use this method when knitting the two-needle sock recipe or variations. It's the same as knitting a regular flat tension/gauge square (**f**).

1. With 3.75mm (US5) needles and double knitting (DK/8ply) weight yarn, cast on approximately 30 stitches.

2. Work 4 rows in garter stitch (knit every row).

3. Work in stocking (stockinette) stitch for approximately 11cm (4⅜in).

4. Work 4 rows in garter stitch and cast (bind) off.

5. Block your swatch and leave it to dry flat without stretching it before measuring your tension/gauge.

MEASURING YOUR TENSION/GAUGE

1. Lay your dry swatch on a flat surface.

2. Place a see-through ruler vertically across the stitches and measure 2.5cm (1in) across the centre.

3. Mark the beginning and end with pins.

4. Do the same vertically and place pins as markers.

5. Count how many stitches there are between the horizontal pins; count how many rows there are between the vertical pins. This tells you how many stitches and rows there are to 2.5cm (1in).

Using an example

For my tension/gauge sample I used 4ply (fingering) sock yarn and knitted a tube, I counted 8 stitches and 11 rows to measure 2.5 x 2.5cm (1 x 1in) using 2.5mm (US2 or US1) needles over stocking (stockinette) stitch worked in the round.

This is a good tension/gauge to achieve for your knitted socks and is commonly used in sock knitting patterns. This can be referred to as 8 sts per inch, or if you divide 8 stitches by 2.5cm, it would be 3.2 stitches per centimetre.

Many patterns give tension/gauge over 10 x 10cm (4 x 4in), and to compare our measurements to that, we can multiply the stitches counted in 2.5cm (1in) by 4.

For my 8 stitches and 11 rows, this equates to:

32 sts and 44 rows to measure 10 x 10cm (4 x 4in) using 2.5mm (US2 or US1) needles over stocking (stockinette) stitch worked in the round.

But don't worry if your tension/gauge is different to mine.

Simply write down the tension/gauge you achieve over 2.5cm (1in) and then multiply this by 4 to get the 10 x 10cm (4 x 4in) tension/gauge.

If you use this tension/gauge along with your sock measurements, you can now use the following chart to work out which sock size to knit.

The first rows of this chart show my tension/gauge, but I've left blank lines for you to use your own tension/gauge to work out how many stitches you would need to cast on and which size of sock is nearest to this.

From the table you will first work out the actual circumference to knit and for this you will need to measure your foot circumference (see All about socks: Measuring foot size).

$(A) - (B) = (C)$

Then you will multiply (C) by (D) to get (E) to see the nearest sock size to knit from.

Most sock patterns follow standard sizes, casting on either 56 [60] [64] [68] [72] stitches. However, it is worth noting that these cast-on numbers may sometimes be slightly different, depending on the sock design itself. Make sure to check the tension/gauge and finished measurements given in the specific pattern you are using.

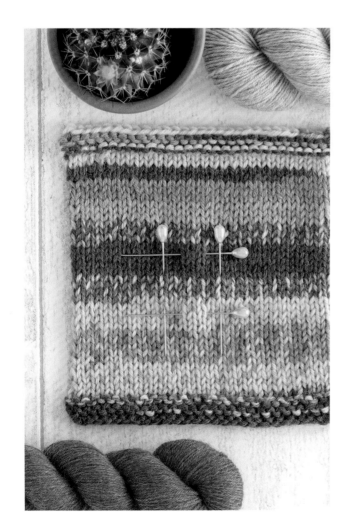

(A) Measured foot circumference (cm or in)	(B) Negative ease (5%) (cm or in)	(C) Actual knitted circumference including negative ease (cm or in)	(D) Measured tension/gauge (stitches per cm or stitches per in)	(E) Calculated cast on stitches needed (rounded to nearest whole number)	Nearest sock size to use (select from: 56 [60] [64] [68] [72] stitches or as per your chosen pattern)
Calculated in cm					
18.5cm	0.9cm	17.6cm	3.2 per cm	56	56
20cm	1cm	19cm	3.2 per cm	61	60
21cm	1.05cm	19.95cm	3.2 per cm	64	64
22.5cm	1.1cm	21.4cm	3.2 per cm	68	68
23.5cm	1.2cm	22.3cm	3.2 per cm	71	72
Calculated in inches					
7¼in	0.36in	6.89in	8 per in	55	56
7¾in	0.39in	7.36in	8 per in	59	60
8¼in	0.41in	7.84in	8 per in	63	64
8¾in	0.44in	8.31in	8 per in	67	68
9¼in	0.46in	8.79in	8 per in	70	72
Your calculations for your measured foot and tension/gauge					

ACHIEVING TENSION/GAUGE IN A PATTERN

A designer will specify the tension/gauge to use in their pattern, so you will need to check that your tension/gauge matches this by knitting a swatch and measuring it as explained in Swatching.

If your stitch and row counts are the same as specified, you can go ahead and start knitting.

If you have **more** stitches than the given tension/gauge, you are knitting too tightly and your sock circumference will end up too small. You'll need to make another swatch with slightly larger needles and measure again.

If you have **fewer** stitches than the given tension/gauge, you are knitting too loosely and your sock circumference will be too big. You'll need to make another swatch with slightly smaller needles and measure again.

Continue to swatch with different sized needles until you achieve the correct tension/gauge stated, and make sure that you always use this needle size for the main part of your socks.

If you can't match both the stitch and row tension/gauge, then go with the closest needles you can match the **stitch** tension/gauge with, since you can adjust the length of the leg and foot of the sock by knitting more or fewer rows.

SOCK RECIPES

Now that you've read through the basics, you are ready to either cast on and knit your first pair of socks, or try a new type of sock knitting technique. I have provided 3 basic recipes in a simple step-by-step format to get you started on your sock knitting adventures. I have chosen elements that are nice and easy, and for added support there is a full techniques section at the end of the book with lots of beautifully illustrated tutorials. With all of this information to hand, you'll be knitting socks in no time at all.

GETTING STARTED

These sock recipes will walk you step-by-step through the process of knitting a basic sock. You can choose to work cuff-down, toe-up or even work a two-needle sock (knitting flat). For simplicity and to get you started on your sock knitting journey, each of the recipes are first knitted in just one colour of yarn.

This is sometimes called a 'vanilla sock', a phrase used a lot within the sock knitting community. But this label can be a little misleading as there is so much beauty to behold in knitting with the same yarn throughout, especially if you choose a speckled, variegated or self-striping yarn – the beauty of a sock often lies within the yarn itself. This could be the rich depth of colour, the light and dark of a tonal yarn, or the pretty speckles of a hand-dyed yarn.

Knitting a simple sock can help your yarn to shine, without any fancy stitches or stitch patterns, and if you only ever knitted a 'vanilla' sock forever, I doubt that you would get bored as there are so many amazing yarns out there for socks (see Tools and materials: Yarn).

Once you have mastered one or more of these recipes, you can then read how to mix and match different cuffs, heels, toes or even add a few stripes (see Variations on the sock recipes).

You may need to knit a few pairs of socks before you decide on your preferred methods of working, but whichever methods you use, each sock will become a mini work of art and you will be able to wear them with pride.

Before you begin

Check that your tension/gauge is correct to the recipe you choose (see Checking your tension/gauge). Continue throughout to use whatever size needles you need to achieve the given tension/gauge.

Check your foot size (see All about socks: Measuring foot size) in order to work out which sock size to knit, according to the circumference of your foot. Five sizes are included, ranging from child/pre-teen through to large adult, with the smallest size given first, followed by larger sizes in brackets. Choose from XS [S] [M] [L] [XL] and follow instructions for your chosen size throughout.

And here are some extra tips before you begin:

- Yarn amounts will vary depending on the size of socks you choose to knit but 100g (3.5oz) will usually be more than enough. For smaller sizes it is sometimes possible to knit 2 pairs of socks from one 100g (3.5oz) ball of sock yarn.

- Remember that socks are knitted with negative ease so they are smaller than your actual foot circumference. They will stretch to fit (see All about socks: Choosing the correct size).

- Remember that the circumference of your foot is the critical factor and not your shoe size as you can knit the foot to any length.

- If you need to brush up on your skills, see Sock techniques.

- It may help to highlight your chosen size throughout for ease of reading.

Cuff-down socks

This tutorial uses the traditional method of knitting in the round with double-pointed needles (DPNs) and I have joined to work in the round using my favourite technique, which doesn't create a gap or a visible jog where the round joins.

You will need

Yarn
1 x 100g (3.5oz) ball/skein of 4ply (fingering) yarn that is approximately 400m (437 yards) in length per ball/skein

OR

2 x 50g (1.75oz) balls/skeins of 4ply (fingering) yarn that is approximately 200m (218 yards) in length per ball/skein

Needles
A set of five 2.5mm (US2 or US1) double-pointed needles (DPNs) (see Tools and materials: Needles)

Extras
3 removable stitch markers; tape measure or ruler; stitch holder (optional); tapestry/yarn needle (for weaving in ends); pair of sock blockers (optional), towel and wool wash for blocking (see Tools and materials: Extras)

Tension/Gauge
32 sts and 44 rows to 10 x 10cm (4 x 4in) measured in stocking (stockinette) stitch using 2.5mm (US2 or US1) needles (see Checking your tension/gauge)

If you need to use a different needle size to achieve this tension, make sure that you use this size throughout.

Sizes
XS [S] [M] [L] [XL]

Knitted sock, actual knitted circumference:
17.5 [19] [20] [21.5] [22.5]cm (6¾ [7½] [8] [8½] [8¾]in)

Will stretch to fit approximate foot circumference:
18.5 [20] [21] [22.5] [23.5]cm (7¼ [8] [8¼] [8¾] [9¼]in)

Abbreviations
DPN(s), double-pointed needle(s); **k**, knit; **k2tog**, knit 2 stitches together, to decrease 1 stitch; **knitwise**, insert needle as if to knit; **p**, purl; **p2tog**, purl 2 stitches together, to decrease 1 stitch; **purlwise**, insert needle as if to purl; **RS**, right side; **skpo**, slip 1 stitch knitwise, knit 1 stitch, pass slipped stitch over the knitted stitch, to decrease 1 stitch; **st(s)**, stitch(es)

The process

First you will cast on and work a 2 x 2 rib cuff in the round, followed by a stocking (stockinette) stitch leg. Then you will knit a slipstitch heel flap, turn the heel, work the instep and shape the gusset. After knitting the foot in stocking (stockinette) stitch, you will shape the classic wedge toe before closing the toe stitches with Kitchener stitch.

All of these steps are commonly used in cuff-down sock knitting and are explained here step-by-step so you can complete your own cuff-down sock as you follow along.

Both of these pairs are knitted with this cuff-down recipe – the different yarn makes them both shine in their own way!

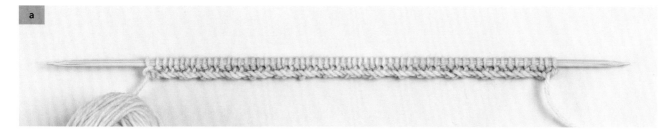

CASTING ON AND JOINING IN THE ROUND

1. Onto 1 DPN and with your chosen method (see Sock techniques: Casting on), cast on 56 [60] [64] [68] [72] sts.

2. Using a second DPN, work the first round of 2 x 2 rib as follows:

Rib round: (K2, p2) to the end. Do not turn your work (keep RS of knitting facing you) (**a**).

Knitting 1 round first will make your stitches easier to manoeuvre around your needles.

3. Starting at the right-hand side of the DPN (at the opposite end to the working yarn), and keeping RS facing at all times, slide the first 14 [15] [16] [17] [18] sts onto 1 DPN (this is called Needle 4); slide the next 14 [15] [16] [17] [18] sts onto the next DPN (this is called Needle 3); slide the next 14 [15] [16] [17] [18] sts onto the next DPN (this is called Needle 2) and leave the final 14 [15] [16] [17] [18] sts on the original DPN (this is now called Needle 1) (**b**).

4. Now you will prepare to start knitting in the round. Keeping RS facing, carefully bring the tips of Needle 4 and Needle 1 around together and slide the stitches up to the top of the needles so they are ready to be knitted and join to start working in the round.

Note: It is important to check that your stitches are not twisted around your needles before you join to work in the round, otherwise your knitting will have a permanent twist in it.

5. I like to use the technique which connects the stitches and doesn't leave any gaps, as follows:

Insert the tip of the right-hand needle (Needle 4) purlwise into the top stitch on Needle 1, slide it off the needle and onto Needle 4, insert the tip of Needle 1 purlwise into the second stitch on Needle 4, lift this stitch up and over the top stitch and onto Needle 1.

The stitches are now crossed and the top stitch on Needle 1 is now the first stitch of the round (**c**). This joining technique is also illustrated in detail in Knitting in the round: Joining the round.

If you find Step 5 tricky, you can jump straight to the cuff. At the end, fix any small gap at the join using the tail end of yarn to sew a few stitches to close it when weaving in ends.

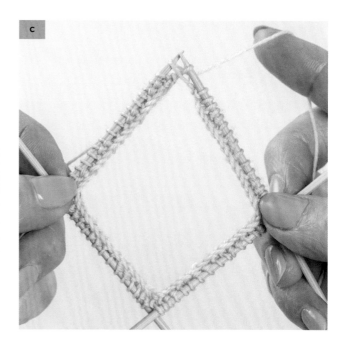

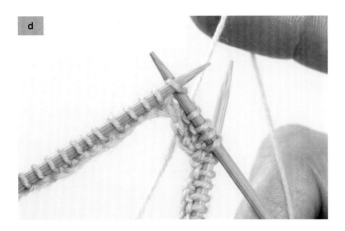

THE CUFF

1. Using your spare DPN, start knitting the stitches on Needle 1 in the same rib pattern as before (repeating Rib round), pulling your working yarn tight before knitting the first 2 stitches (**d**).

Knitting with DPNs may seem tricky at first, but the key is to try to ignore the other needles as if they weren't there.

When Needle 1 then becomes free, use this to knit the stitches off the next needle. and so on. When you have knitted the stitches off Needle 4, you have completed the round. You should begin to see neat columns of rib stitch appearing and the rib should start to feel more flexible and stretchy as you knit more and more rounds.

Note: When you knit the first stitch off each DPN, it's important to pull the yarn tight before knitting, so that your tension/gauge isn't loose on the end stitches. Otherwise you will see a visible line in your knitting where loose stitches will stand out – but don't worry if this happens, blocking your socks will help to minimize this (see Sock techniques: Finishing your project)

2. Use a stitch marker to identify the start of the round (**e**). Stitch markers can fall off the end of DPNs, so it may be more practical to use a removable stitch marker placed in the first or last stitch of the round and move it up after every few rounds.

3. Continue to repeat Rib round until you have worked 20 rounds of rib in total (or the length you desire – you can work less rounds if you prefer). You will finish at the end of the round which is the centre back of your sock (**f**).

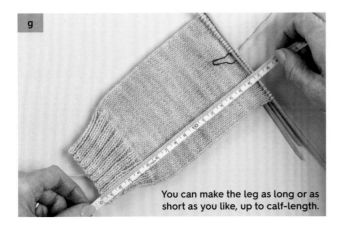

THE LEG

1. To start knitting the leg, change to stocking (stockinette) stitch (knit every round). Work in stocking (stockinette) stitch until your sock measures approximately 16.5cm (6½in), or shorter if desired (**g**).

Remember to move your stitch marker up as you work the leg.

You can make the leg as long or as short as you like, up to calf-length.

THE HEEL FLAP

1. Remove the start of the round stitch marker while working the heel flap. You will now start working in rows using 2 of your DPNs only, knitting back and forth, turning after each row. I've chosen a slipstitch heel flap and gusset for this sock (see Sock elements: Heels).

Set-up row 1 (RS): K14 [15] [16] [17] [18], turn.

Set-up row 2: P28 [30] [32] [34] [36], turn.

2. Now you have half of your stitches on 1 DPN ready to knit the heel. These are called the heel stitches. Leave the remaining stitches on your original needles (Needles 2 and 3). These stitches are called the instep (top of foot) stitches, but you will ignore these stitches while you work the heel (**h**).

Note: It is important that you slip the first stitch of each row as stated below, because this will ensure that you only have 1 visible end stitch for every 2 rows of knitting.

Heel row 1 (RS): Slip the first st *knitwise*, k1, *slip the next st *purlwise* (keeping yarn at back), k1; repeat from * to end of heel sts, turn.

Heel row 2: Slip the first st *purlwise* (with yarn at front), then purl every st to end of heel sts, turn.

3. Repeat Heel row 1 and Heel row 2 for a further 12 [13] [14] [15] [16] times.

You now have a rectangular heel flap with 13 [14] [15] [16] [17] slipped sts along each side edge (**i**).

These edge stitches will appear slightly elongated and should be easy to count. You will use them later when picking up the gusset stitches.

When you slip every alternate stitch on the right side rows, the short strands of yarn sit across the back of the slipped stitches and form a double layer of fabric that is hard wearing (**j**).

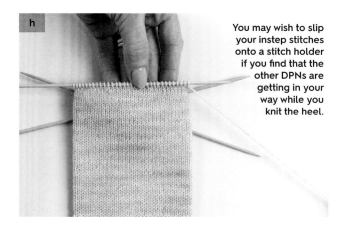

You may wish to slip your instep stitches onto a stitch holder if you find that the other DPNs are getting in your way while you knit the heel.

THE HEEL TURN

1. Work short rows as follows (this isn't difficult, it just means that you don't work all of the stitches along the row before turning):

Row 1 (RS): Slip 1 st *knitwise*, k15 [16] [17] [18] [19], skpo, k1, turn.

Row 2: Slip 1 st *purlwise*, p5, p2tog, p1, turn.

There is a visible gap between the stitches knitted and the stitches waiting to be worked; use this as a marker for the following rows.

Row 3 (RS): Slip 1 st *knitwise*, knit to 1 st before the gap (**k**), skpo (using the st before and the st after the gap), k1, turn.

Row 4: Slip 1 st *purlwise*, purl to 1 st before the gap, p2tog (using the st before and the st after the gap), p1, turn.

2. Repeat Rows 3-4 until all sts have been used up and 16 [18] [18] [20] [20] heel sts remain.

Note that on the final 2 rows for sizes XS [M] [XL] you will miss off the k1 or p1 at the end of each row, so for these sizes, the last 2 rows will read:

Second to last row (RS): Slip 1 st *knitwise*, knit to 1 st before the gap, skpo, turn.

Last row: Slip 1 st *purlwise*, purl to 1 st before the gap, p2tog, turn.

For all sizes, your yarn is situated at the right-hand side of the remaining heel sts. This is the new start of round (**l**).

PICKING UP THE GUSSET STITCHES

1. Now you will connect the heel back to the instep stitches, by picking up stitches along each side of the heel flap and knitting across the instep stitches. You will have a lot more stitches than you started with originally, but you will start to decrease these extra stitches on each side of the instep to shape the gusset.

With RS of work facing, knit across the remaining 16 [18] [18] [20] [20] heel sts (Needle 1), with next DPN pick up and knit 13 [14] [15] [16] [17] sts along the first edge of the heel flap, inserting tip of needle into the first slipped stitch of each heel row and underneath both loops of the stitch (**m**) (see Sock techniques: Picking up stitches).

When you reach the end of the heel flap you will see a visible gap between the stitch just picked up and the instep stitches. To close this gap, pick up an extra stitch by using the M1R method (**n**) (see Sock techniques: Increasing).

2. With next DPN knit 28 [30] [32] [34] [36] instep (front) sts off the next 2 DPNs, placing a removable stitch marker in the first stitch and last stitch on this needle. All of your front (instep) stitches are now on Needle 3 and you will have a removable stitch marker marking the first and last instep sts.

With next DPN, pick up and knit 1 st from gap before heel flap by using the M1L method (see Sock techniques: Increasing).

Finally, with same DPN, pick up and knit 13 [14] [15] [16] [17] sts along the next edge of the heel flap. (There are 14 [15] [16] [17] [18] sts on Needle 4.)

You now have 72 [78] [82] [88] [92] sts in total and have reached the end of the round. Needles 1, 2 and 4 hold the sole (bottom of foot) sts and Needle 3 holds the instep (top of foot) sts.

Place another removable stitch marker in the first st on Needle 1 to mark the new start of the round (**o**).

Note: The start of round position has now changed to sit on one side of the heel. This is a good place to start each round because if you decide to work in stripes or colourwork then you will carry yarn along the inside of your sock at this point. With the start of round on the underside of your foot then you may feel the strands of yarn and colour changes, and this would be uncomfortable on the sole of your foot. However, it's worth noting that sock patterns do vary and some designers keep the start of the round at the centre point of the heel.

GUSSET SHAPING

1. Now you will decrease on each side of the instep stitches as follows:

Round 1: With spare DPN, knit to 3 sts before first stitch marker (this is 3 sts before end of Needle 2) (**p**). Next, k2tog, k1, then with next DPN knit across all stitches on Needle 3 including the marked stitches (these are the instep stitches). With next DPN k1, skpo, knit to end of round (to end of Needle 4). (2 sts decreased)

The markers show the end stitches of the front (instep) and the position of the decrease stitches.

Round 2: Knit all sts to end of round.

2. Repeat the last 2 rounds until 56 [60] [64] [68] [72] sts remain, ending after a Round 1 (**q**).

Make sure that you have moved up all your stitch markers and continue to move them up every 2 rounds.

THE FOOT

1. Continue in stocking (stockinette) stitch (knit every round) until sock measures approximately 4 [4] [4.5] [4.5] [5]cm (1½ [1½] [1¾] [1¾] [2]in) less than the desired foot length (**r**) (see All about socks: Choosing the correct size).

2. Remove the start of the round stitch marker and knit up to the next stitch marker. This is now the new start of the round.

Manoeuvre your stitches around so that the top stitches are on Needles 1 and 2, and the bottom stitches are on Needles 3 and 4.

THE TOE

1. Work a classic wedge toe, following the instructions for your size below.

Round 1: *K1, skpo, knit to 3 sts before next marker, k2tog, k1; repeat from * once more. (4 sts decreased)

Round 2: Knit all sts to end of round and slip both markers.

2. Repeat Rounds 1-2 until 20 [24] [24] [28] [28] sts remain and remove stitch markers (**s**).

GRAFTING WITH KITCHENER STITCH

1. Join the toe stitches together using Kitchener stitch (also called grafting) by weaving yarn through the stitches, following **Steps 2-8** below (also see Sock techniques: Finishing your project).

2. To set up, hold the remaining sts on 2 DPNs parallel, with wrong sides of knitting facing each other and right sides facing outwards, and with the sts attached to the working yarn on the back needle. Cut the working yarn, leaving a long tail end and thread onto a tapestry/yarn needle.

3. Insert tapestry/yarn needle into first st on front needle *purlwise* (**t**). Pull yarn through, leaving st on the needle.

4. Insert tapestry/yarn needle into first st on back needle *knitwise* (**u**). Pull yarn through, leaving st on the needle.

5. Insert tapestry/yarn needle into the first st on the front needle *knitwise* and slip it off the end of the needle (**v**).

6. Insert the tapestry/yarn needle into the next st on the front needle *purlwise*. Pull yarn through and this time leave st on the needle (as you did in Step 3).

7. Insert tapestry/yarn needle into the first st on the back needle *purlwise*, and slip it off the end of the needle (**w**).

8. Repeat **Steps 4-7** until all sts have been grafted together, stopping regularly to tighten up the stitches to create a tension (gauge) that matches your knitting.

When you reach the end of your stitches, insert your tapestry/yarn needle down into the sock to the inside, through the middle of the next stitch on the main sock.

FINISHING

1. Weave in the start and end tails of yarn and trim (see Sock techniques: Finishing your project – Weaving in ends).

Soak socks in cold water with wool wash for 10 minutes, then carefully squeeze out water (do not wring). Roll in a towel to press out excess water then place on sock blockers, or leave flat to dry (see Sock techniques: Finishing your project – Blocking your project).

VARIATIONS

Once you have got to grips with the various techniques you can mix and match different cuffs, heels and toes, and even try some colourful stripes too (see Variations on the sock recipes).

Toe-up socks

This recipe will walk you step-by-step through knitting a toe-up sock with a basic wrap and turn heel, which uses short rows to create a neat, knitted pocket for your heel. It uses the magic loop method of knitting in the round with a long circular needle. It begins with a closed cast on and ends with a super stretchy cast (bind) off. You can switch for your own preferred heel or cuff, or even work the heel in a contrast colour (see Variations on the sock recipes).

You will need

Yarn
1 x 100g (3.5oz) ball/skein of 4ply (fingering) yarn that is approximately 400m (437 yards) in length per ball/skein

OR

2 x 50g (1.75oz) balls/skeins of 4ply (fingering) yarn that is approximately 200m (218 yards) in length per ball/skein

Needles
A long circular knitting needle 2.5mm (US2 or US1) and a pair of 2.5mm (US2 or US1) DPNs (see Tools and materials: Needles)

Extras
Tape measure or ruler; stitch markers; stitch holder (optional); tapestry/yarn needle (for weaving in ends); pair of sock blockers (optional), towel and wool wash for blocking (see Tools and materials: Extras)

Tension/Gauge
32 sts and 44 rows to 10 x 10cm (4 x 4in) measured in stocking (stockinette) stitch using 2.5mm (US2 or US1) needles (see Checking your tension/gauge)

If you need to use a different needle size to achieve this tension/gauge, make sure that you use this size throughout.

Sizes
XS [S] [M] [L] [XL]

Knitted sock, actual knitted circumference:
17.5 [19] [20] [21.5] [22.5]cm (6¾ [7½] [8] [8½] [8¾]in)

Will stretch to fit approximate foot circumference:
18.5 [20] [21] [22.5] [23.5]cm (7¼ [8] [8¼] [8¾] [9¼]in)

Abbreviations
DPN(s), double-pointed needle(s); **k**, knit; **kfb**, knit into the front and then the back of the next stitch, to increase 1 stitch; **knitwise**, insert needle as if to knit; **p**, purl; **purlwise**, insert needle as if to purl; **RS**, right side; **st(s)**, stitch(es); **W&T**, wrap and turn; **WS**, wrong side; **yo**, yarn over, to increase 1 stitch

The process

First you will cast on using a method called 'Judy's magic cast on'. This is a great way to start a toe-up sock because it's a closed cast on which means that the toe stitches are joined as you cast on, therefore forming a seamless start to your sock. Next, you will increase to shape the toe section and continue to knit the foot. Then you will knit a wrap and turn heel and continue with the leg before finishing with the 2 x 2 rib cuff. Finally, you will work a super stretchy cast (bind) off so that the cuff is nice and stretchy around your leg.

All of these steps are commonly used in toe-up sock knitting and are explained here step-by-step so you can complete your own toe-up sock as you follow along.

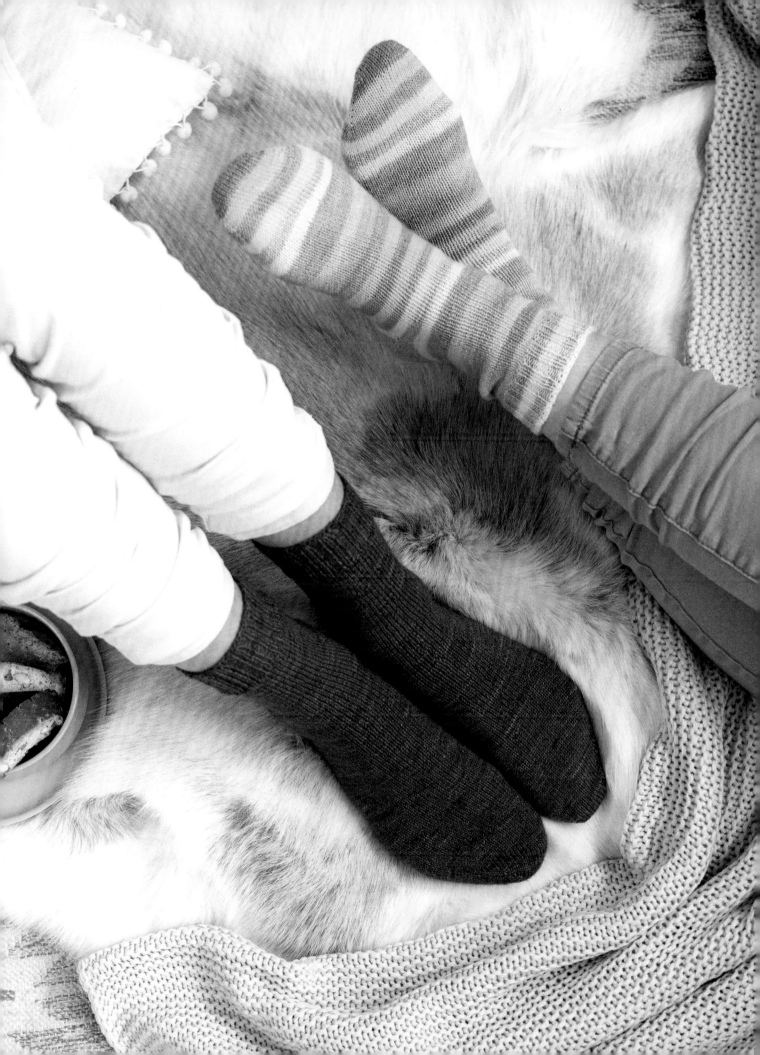

CASTING ON FOR THE TOE

With your long circular needle, and using Judy's magic cast on method, cast on 20 [24] [24] [28] [28] sts over the 2 needle tips – 10 [12] [12] [14] [14] sts on each needle tip, following the steps below.

Also see Sock techniques: Casting on, for an illustrated guide for Judy's magic cast on.

1. Leaving a long tail end of yarn, of approximately 30cm (12in), make a slip knot and place it onto 1 of the needle tips then hold 2 needle tips in your right hand, alongside each another, with the slip knot on the top needle and the yarn ends sitting behind the bottom needle.

2. Grab the yarn ends in the palm of your left hand – and insert your first finger and thumb in between the strands of yarn to separate them, with the tail end of yarn over your first finger and the yarn from the ball over your thumb (**a**).

3. Using your right hand to create a figure-of-eight motion, take the tip of the bottom needle to the right and over, and then under, the tail end of yarn (**b**). This will wrap the yarn around the bottom needle. The yarn is now located at the back, between the 2 needles.

4. Next, take the tip of the back needle to the left and over, and then under, the working end of yarn which will wrap the yarn around the top needle. The yarn is once again located at the back, between the 2 needles (**c**).

5. Repeat **Step 3** to cast on 1 more st onto the bottom needle. 2 sts are now on each needle.

6. Repeat **Steps 4 and 5** for as many sts as you need for your chosen size, making sure that you have the same number of sts on each needle.

7. Rotate the needles so that they are pointing to the right, in the correct direction ready to knit (**d**). There is a small row of purl bumps which should sit on the back of the stitches and these indicate the wrong side of your knitting. Top needle is Needle 1 and bottom needle is Needle 2. The working yarn should be at the tip side of Needle 2.

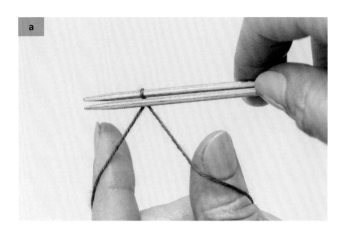

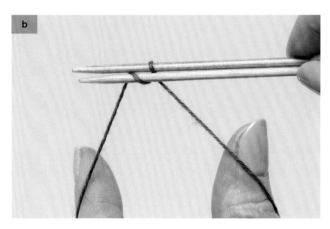

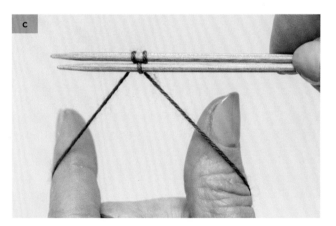

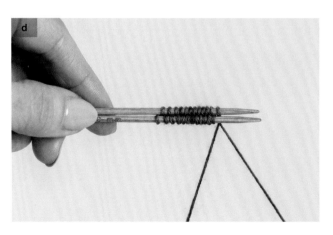

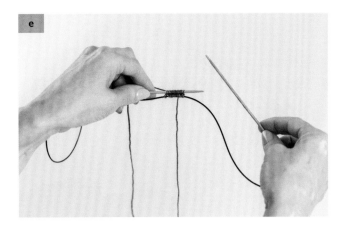

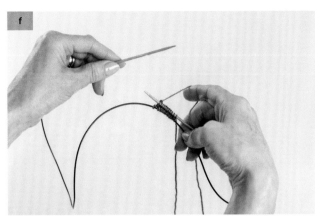

THE TOE

1. To start knitting with magic loop method, gently pull out the tip of Needle 2 and let the cast-on sts slide onto the needle cord (**e**). Pull out enough slack on the cord to knit comfortably, but don't pull the cord out completely otherwise all of your sts will end up on 1 needle. You are ready to work Round 1.

Round 1: Knit all sts to end of round, following the steps below.

2. Use Needle 2 to knit all the sts to the end of Needle 1 (**f**).

3. Rotate needles so that the remaining cast-on sts on the cord are at the top and gently push the tip of Needle 1 back into the sts that are sitting on the cord.

4. Gently pull out the tip of Needle 2 (now back at the bottom) so that the sts you just worked are sitting on the needle cord (**g**), then knit all sts off Needle 1 onto Needle 2 again. You can read more about this method in Knitting in the round: On a long circular needle for magic loop.

5. Rotate needles so that Needle 1 is back at the top, gently push the needle tip back into the sts. Your first round is complete.

6. Add a removable stitch marker to the first or last stitch of the round so that you know when you've completed each round.

7. Now continue to knit with the magic loop method and increase as follows:

Round 2: *Needle 1:* Kfb, knit to last st of Needle 1, kfb; *Needle 2:* kfb, knit to last st of round, kfb. (24 [28] [28] [32] [32] sts)

Round 3: Knit all sts to end of round.

Repeat Rounds 2-3 until you have 56 [60] [64] [68] [72] sts in total (**h**).

> *Slightly tug the yarn before you knit the first stitch on each needle, so that you don't create little gaps or ladders along the sides of your socks.*

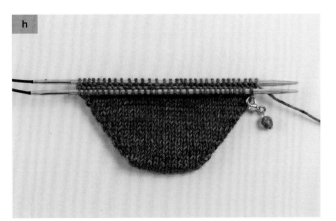

THE FOOT

1. Continue in stocking (stockinette) stitch in the round (knit every round).

2. Work until the sock measures 3.5 [4] [4.5] [4.5] [5]cm (1⅜ [1⅝] [1¾] [1¾] [2]in) less than your total desired foot length, measuring from the toe cast-on (**i**).

This is where your foot template would be really useful! (see All about socks: Measuring foot size)

THE HEEL

You will now work in rows over the first half of your sts only for the heel, which is 28 [30] [32] [34] [36] sts. It's easier if you switch to 2 DPNs to do this.

1. Leave the other half of your sts on your circular needle and slide them onto the cord. These sts are called the instep (top of foot) sts, but you will ignore these sts while you work the heel.

The wrap and turn (W&T) short rows create a neat, defined diagonal line across the heel. If you need to brush up on how to work W&T, see Sock techniques: Short rows.

2. Work the first half of the heel flat on the pair of DPNs as follows:

Row 1 (RS): Knit to last heel st, work a RS W&T as follows: *bring yarn to front between needles, slip next stitch *purlwise* from left-hand to right-hand needle, take yarn back between needles, return slip stitch to left-hand needle, turn work* (**j**).

Row 2: Purl to last heel st, work a WS W&T as follows: **take yarn to back between needles, slip next stitch *purlwise* from left-hand to right-hand needle, bring yarn to front between needles, return slip stitch to left-hand needle, turn work** (**k**).

Row 3: Knit to 1 st before the last wrapped st of the heel, work a RS W&T (repeat from * to * in Row 1).

Row 4: Purl to 1 st before the last wrapped st of the heel, work a WS W&T (repeat from ** to ** in Row 2).

Repeat Rows 3-4 until 8 [10] [10] [10] [12] sts remain unworked in the middle of the heel between the wrapped sts (**l**). The first half of the heel is now complete.

Note that the central unworked sts in (l) have been placed onto a separate DPN for visual purposes only so that you can see them clearly. In your knitting the unworked stitches will be on the left-hand DPN.

3. Continue on the DPNs to complete the second half of the heel as follows:

Some of your sts will end up with a double wrap (2 sts around the base of the stitch) and this really helps to keep the heel seam nice and neat, and without looking loose or holey. If you need to brush up on how to pick up wraps, see Sock techniques: Short rows.

Row 1 (RS): Knit to first wrapped st, pick up wrapped st and knit it together with st on needle (**m**), W&T the next st (this stitch now has 2 wraps at its base (**n**)).

Row 2: Purl to first wrapped st, pick up wrapped st and purl it together with st on needle, W&T the next st (this stitch now has 2 wraps at its base).

Row 3: Knit to st with double wrap. Pick up both wraps and knit them together with st on needle, W&T the next st.

Row 4: Purl to st with double wrap. Pick up both wraps and purl them together with st on needle, W&T the next st.

Repeat Rows 3-4 until there is 1 double wrapped st remaining on each side of heel (**o**).

Next row: Repeat Row 3, working the last W&T on the next st from instep sts on circular needle.

Next row: Repeat Row 4, working the last W&T on the next st from instep sts on circular needle.

4. The heel is now complete (**p**) and you are ready to work the leg.

THE LEG

1. With RS now facing, begin to knit all sts of sock in the round again on the circular needle and using magic loop (**q**). When you come to the final wrapped sts on the instep (the ones just worked on last 2 rows of the heel), pick up these wraps and knit them together with their respective sts (**r**).

These last wraps can be quite tight so you may need to use a tapestry/yarn needle to pick up the wraps.

2. Continue to work in stocking (stockinette) stitch by knitting every round, until sock measures 12.5 [14] [15] [15.5] [16.5]cm (5 [5½] [6] [6¼] [6½]in), measuring from bottom of the heel (**s**).

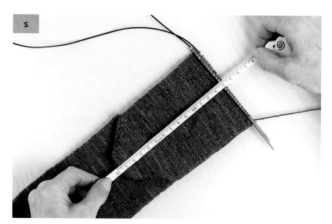

THE CUFF

Rib round: (K2, p2) to end.

Repeat Rib round for a further 15 or 19 times, depending on how deep you would like your cuff (**t**).

CASTING (BINDING) OFF

For toe-up socks, a super stretchy cast (bind) off is recommended so the cuff is stretchy enough to fit over your foot. I find the best results with Jeny's surprisingly stretchy cast (bind) off which I use here (or see Sock techniques: Casting (binding) off, for an illustrated guide).

Cast (bind) off all sts in pattern using a stretchy method, following the steps below for 2 x 2 rib using Jeny's surprisingly stretchy cast (bind) off.

1. Knit first st.

2. Work a backwards yarn over, taking yarn over the needle anti-clockwise (counter-clockwise) from back to front, to back again (**u**). Knit the next st. 3 sts are now on right-hand needle.

3. Lift the bottom 2 sts over the top st to cast (bind) off (**v**), leaving 1 st on right-hand needle.

4. Bring yarn to the front and around needle (**w**) (to create a yarn over), purl next stitch.

5. Lift the bottom 2 sts over the top st to cast (bind) off, leaving 1 st on right-hand needle, yarn over, purl next stitch, lift the bottom 2 sts over the top st to cast (bind) off, leaving 1 st on right-hand needle.

6. Take yarn to the back between the needles, work a backwards yarn over (**u**), then knit the next stitch, lift the bottom 2 sts over the top st to cast (bind) off, leaving 1 st on right-hand needle.

7. Repeat **Steps 2-6** until the end, noting that you will finish casting (binding) off after working the final purl sts.

8. Lengthen the last loop on your needle and cut working yarn. Thread yarn tail onto tapestry/yarn needle and thread it from the back to front through the first cast (bind) off stitch. Thread tapestry/yarn needle through the long loop (**x**) and gently pull to join the stitches of the round. Thread tapestry/yarn needle down through the centre of next cast (bind) off stitch and to the inside of your work.

This stretchy cast (bind) off method uses more yarn because of the extra yarn overs that are being made. Make sure that you account for this when deciding how long to make your socks, ensuring you have at least 4 times the circumference of your finished sock remaining of your yarn before you begin the cast (bind) off.

FINISHING

1. Weave in the start and end tails of yarn and trim (see Sock techniques: Finishing your project).

2. Soak socks in cold water with wool wash for 10 minutes, then carefully squeeze out water (do not wring). Roll in a towel to press out excess water then place on sock blockers, or leave flat to dry (see Sock techniques: Finishing your project).

VARIATIONS

Once you have got to grips with the various techniques you can mix and match different cuffs, heels and toes, and even try some colourful stripes too (see Variations on the sock recipes).

Two-needle socks

I find it amazing that these finished two-needle socks look almost identical to a sock that is worked in the round, but instead they're knitted flat and seamed. They use some of the same techniques and elements, but the difference is that these are knitted with straight needles and are therefore the perfect solution if you're longing to knit a pair of socks, but you really don't like knitting in the round. I've made this pair with thicker yarn, so they're very quick to make.

You will need

Yarn
1 x 150g (5.3oz) ball/skein of 6ply yarn that is approximately 375m (410 yards) in length per ball/skein

OR

You can use thin double knitting (DK/8ply) yarn that is approximately 250m (275 yards) in length per 100g (3.5oz) ball/skein, or 2 balls approximately 125m (130 yards) in length per 50g (1.75oz) ball/skein

Needles
A pair of 3.75mm (US5) straight knitting needles and a pair of 3.75mm (US5) DPNs or cable needles (for holding sts) (see Tools and materials: Needles)

Extras
Tape measure or ruler; 3 stitch holders; removable stitch marker or spare yarn; tapestry/yarn needle (for weaving in ends); pair of sock blockers (optional), towel and wool wash for blocking (see Tools and materials: Extras)

Tension/Gauge
24 sts and 32 rows to 10 x 10cm (4 x 4in) measured in stocking (stockinette) stitch using 3.75mm (US5) needles (see Checking your tension/gauge)

If you need to use a different needle size to achieve this tension/gauge, make sure that you use this size throughout.

Sizes
XS [S] [M] [L] [XL]

Knitted sock, actual knitted circumference:
17.5 [19] [20] [21.5] [22.5]cm (6¾ [7½] [8] [8½] [8¾]in)

Will stretch to fit approximate foot circumference:
18.5 [20] [21] [22.5] [23.5]cm (7¼ [8] [8¼] [8¾] [9¼]in)

Abbreviations
DPN(s), double-pointed needle(s); **k**, knit; **k2tog**, knit 2 stitches together, to decrease 1 stitch; **knitwise**, insert needle as if to knit; **p**, purl; **p2tog**, purl 2 stitches together, to decrease 1 stitch; **purlwise**, insert needle as if to purl; **RS**, right side; **skpo**, slip 1 stitch knitwise, knit 1 stitch, pass slipped stitch over the knitted stitch, to decrease 1 stitch; **st(s)**, stitch(es)

The process

First you will cast on and work a 1 x 1 rib in rows, followed by the leg. The upper foot (instep) is worked first on the centre stitches, then you will shape the upper toe. Then the remaining stitches are worked when you knit a slipstitch heel flap, turn the heel, then work the sole, including shaping the gusset. After knitting the foot in rows in stocking (stockinette) stitch, you will shape the underside of the toe before seaming the toe stitches with three-needle cast (bind) off. Finally, you will sew the back seam of the cuff and leg, and the side seams of the gusset, foot and toe, using mattress stitch. This method of knitting and seaming creates a back seam on the leg and 2 side seams running along the sides of the foot, for balance and comfort.

All of these steps are similar to cuff-down sock knitting and are explained here step-by-step so you can complete your own two-needle sock as you follow along.

CUFF

With your straight needles, and with your chosen cast on method, cast on 45 [47] [49] [53] [57] sts (**a**).

I've used the long-tail cast on (see Sock techniques: Casting on). Whichever method you choose, make sure the cast-on edge is stretchy enough to allow the cuff to fit over your foot.

1. Work in 1 x 1 rib as follows:

Rib row 1 (RS): (K1, p1) to the last st, k1.

Rib row 2: (P1, k1) to the last st, p1.

2. Repeat the last 2 rows for a further 5 times, or the length you desire.

You can work less/more rounds of rib if you prefer, just make sure to end after a Rib row 2 (**b**).

THE LEG

1. With RS facing, change to work in stocking (stockinette) stitch (1 row knit, 1 row purl, repeated throughout).

2. Continue in stocking (stockinette) stitch until your sock measures approximately 16.5cm (6½in), or length desired (**c**).

DIVIDE FOR INSTEP AND HEEL

1. K34 [35] [37] [40] [43] sts, place unworked 11 [12] [12] [13] [14] sts onto a stitch holder (**d**).

2. Turn and purl 23 [23] [25] [27] [29] sts for the instep/top of foot.

INSTEP

1. Turn and work on these centre sts only for instep (top of foot), placing remaining 11 [12] [12] [13] [14] sts onto another stitch holder (**e**).

It may help for measuring if you place a removable stitch marker or short length of yarn into a stitch on the last row.

2. Continue straight in stocking (stockinette) stitch until foot length is 8.5 [8.5] [9] [9] [10]cm (3¼ [3¼] [3½] [3½] [4]in) less than the desired foot length (**f**) (see All about socks: Measuring foot size) and make sure that you make a note of the number of rows you have worked to match the sole.

Note: *You are working to a much shorter length because you need to deduct heel and toe measurements from the total foot length.*

THE UPPER TOE

1. Shape the upper toe, decreasing as follows:

Row 1 (RS): K2, skpo, knit to last 4 sts, k2tog, k2. (21 [21] [23] [25] [27] sts)

Row 2: Purl to end.

Repeat Rows 1-2 for a further 5 [5] [6] [6] [7] times. (11 [11] [11] [13] [13] sts)

Next row: Repeat Row 1. (9 [9] [9] [11] [11] sts)

2. Decreases are complete (**g**).

3. Cut yarn, leaving a long tail end. Slip sts onto a DPN or cable needle, noting that you will need to access both ends of this needle (**h**). For now, leave them on hold while you complete the heel.

THE HEEL

1. Place work flat with wrong side uppermost – with toe at the top and rib at the bottom.

2. Fold the 2 sets of sts on stitch holders inwards so that the right sides of the cuff are now facing (**i**).

3. Starting from the left-hand side, slip the 11 [12] [12] [13] [14] sts from the left stitch holder onto 1 DPN.

4. Next, slip the 11 [12] [12] [13] [14] sts from the right stitch holder onto the same DPN (**j**).

5. With right sides facing, you are ready to work across both sets of sts to work the heel as follows:

Row 1 (RS): Join in yarn and knit to last st of first half of heel, k2tog across this stitch and the first st of next half of heel (**k**), knit to end. (21 [23] [23] [25] [27] sts)

Row 2: K3, purl to last 2 sts, k3.

Row 3: Knit to end.

Row 4: K3, purl to last 2 sts, k3.

Repeat Rows 3-4 for a further 6 [7] [8] [8] [9] times (**l**).

6. Turn the heel as follows:

Row 1 (RS): Slip 1 st *knitwise*, k11 [12] [12] [13] [14], skpo, k1, turn.

Row 2: Slip 1 st *purlwise*, p4, p2tog, p1, turn.

7. There is a visible gap between the stitches already knitted and the stitches waiting to be worked (**m**); use this as a marker for the following rows.

Row 3 (RS): Slip 1 st *knitwise*, knit to 1 st before the gap (**n**), skpo (using the st before and the st after the gap), k1, turn.

Row 4: Slip 1 st *purlwise*, purl to 1 st before the gap, p2tog (using the st before and the st after the gap), p1, turn.

Repeat Rows 3-4 until all sts have been used up and 13 [13] [13] [15] [15] heel sts remain.

Note: *On the final 2 rows for size [S] [M] [XL] you will miss off the k1 or p1 at the end of each row, so for these sizes, the last 2 rows will read:*

Second to last row (RS): Slip 1 st *knitwise*, knit to 1 st before the gap, skpo, turn.

Last row: Slip 1 st *purlwise*, purl to 1 st before the gap, p2tog, turn.

8. Your yarn is situated at the right-hand side of the remaining heel sts (**o**). You will need to cut this yarn and re-join it so that you can start the gusset at the bottom of the heel flap (the point marked in (**p**) with a stitch marker).

THE GUSSET

1. Re-joining yarn at beginning of Row 1, set up for the gusset as follows:

Row 1 (RS): With right side facing, pick up and knit 9 [10] [11] [11] [12] sts along right-hand side of heel (**q**), k13 [13] [13] [15] [15] sts from heel, then pick up and knit 9 [10] [11] [11] [12] sts along left-hand side of heel (**r**). (31 [33] [35] [37] [39] sts)

The general rule is to pick up 1 st before the first garter stitch ridge, 1 st in between every garter stitch ridge along the heel edge and 1 st after the last garter stitch ridge.

Row 2: Purl to end.

Row 3: K2, skpo, knit to last 4 sts, k2tog, k2. (29 [31] [33] [35] [37] sts)

Row 4: Purl to end.

Repeat Rows 3-4 until you have 23 [23] [25] [27] [29] sts.

2. The gusset shaping is complete and you will see a neat sloping line of decreases along each edge at the heel end (**s**).

THE SOLE

It may help for measuring if you place a removable stitch marker or short length of yarn into a stitch on the last row of the gusset.

1. Continue in stocking (stockinette) stitch.

2. Work straight until you have knitted the same number of rows as your instep (top of foot) to the toe.

UNDERSIDE OF TOE

1. Shape the underside of toe, decreasing as follows:

Row 1 (RS): K2, skpo, knit to last 4 sts, k2tog, k2. (21 [21] [23] [25] [27] sts)

Row 2: Purl to end.

Repeat Rows 1-2 for a further 5 [5] [6] [6] [7] times. (11 [11] [11] [13] [13] sts)

Next row: Repeat Row 1. (9 [9] [9] [11] [11] sts)

2. Slip sts onto a DPN or cable needle (**t**).

You can now check your sock against your foot and, if needed, adjust by working an extra row or 2 at the toe end on each needle, using the long tail ends of yarn. Remember that the seam will also add an extra row.

JOINING UPPER AND UNDERSIDE OF TOE PIECES

1. Adjust both upper foot and sole pieces so that the right sides are together and the wrong sides are facing outwards, lining up the sts on both needles (**u**).

2. Cast (bind) off both sets of sts together, using the three-needle cast (bind) off method (**v**) (see Sock techniques: Casting (binding) off).

3. Fasten off, leaving a long tail end for sewing seams.

JOINING THE SIDE SEAMS

1. With right sides facing, join each side seam using mattress stitch (**w**) (see Sock techniques: Finishing your project).

2. Join centre back seam using mattress stitch (**x**).

Mattress stitch will leave a flat seam.

3. Weave in all ends and trim (see Sock techniques: Finishing your project).

4. Finally, block your socks and leave to dry completely (see Sock techniques: Finishing your project).

VARIATIONS

Once you have got to grips with the various techniques you can mix and match different cuffs, heels and toes, and even try some colourful stripes too (see Variations on the sock recipes).

VARIATIONS ON THE SOCK RECIPES

Once you've mastered the basics, you might like to try these simple variations to help you create a colourful and assorted hand-knitted sock collection.

'Scrappy' socks are perfect for creating your own colour schemes with all those scraps of leftover yarns and there's even a 'no-heel' sock option for those of you who don't like knitting the heels.

Contrast cuffs, heels and toes

You can easily change the look of a sock by adding contrast yarn for different elements of the sock. It's also a perfect option for using up all those oddments of sock yarn. You can try contrast cuffs, heels and toes or just a contrast heel – the choice is yours entirely.

To use different colours, simply follow your preferred recipe throughout, but change colour for each element as instructed below. For more information on how to change colour, you can also see Sock techniques: Working with more than one yarn/colour.

CONTRAST ELEMENTS IN CUFF-DOWN SOCKS

For the cuff:

Cast on with your contrast colour and knit the full cuff according to the recipe.

Change to main colour to knit the leg.

For the heel:

Change to contrast colour after working **Set-up row 1** of the heel flap.

Continue as instructed to the end of the heel turn.

Change back to the main colour before picking up the gusset sts.

For the toe:

When you have knitted the foot and have manoeuvred your sts ready to work the toe, change to contrast colour for the toe.

CONTRAST ELEMENTS IN TOE-UP SOCKS

For the toe:

Cast on with contrast colour and work the toe increases according to the recipe. If desired, you can knit a few more rounds straight, to make your toe deeper.

Change to main colour to knit the foot.

For the heel:

Change to contrast colour to knit the heel.

Change back to main colour to knit the leg.

For the cuff:

Change to contrast colour to knit the cuff.

CONTRAST ELEMENTS IN TWO-NEEDLE SOCKS

For the cuff:

Cast on with your contrast colour and knit the full cuff according to the recipe.

Change to main colour to knit the leg and the instep.

For the upper toe:

Change to contrast colour to knit the upper toe.

For the heel:

Join with contrast colour to work the heel.

Join with main colour when picking up the gusset sts and work gusset and sole in main colour.

For the underside of the toe:

Change to contrast colour to knit the underside of the toe.

Scrappy socks

For all those oddments of sock yarn.

Follow the basic cuff-down sock or toe-up sock recipe throughout but instead of working in a single colour, working a fixed number of rounds throughout for each colour (for example 7 rounds), or work stripes that vary in depth.

Changing colour to create stripes can lead to a visible 'jog' where the knitted stitches do not line up at the beginning and end of the round. This happens because when you're knitting in the round, you are essentially knitting in a spiral and therefore your first and last stitches do not meet. Instead, the last stitch of the round sits higher than the first stitch of the round. While this is not visible when using the same colour, it shows more when you change colour to knit in stripes. You may not mind the visual appearance of the 'jog' but if you would like to smooth it out you can try working jogless stripes (see Sock techniques: Working with more than one yarn/colour).

You can still work your toes and heels in a single colour if desired, by following the instructions above for contrast elements.

Shortie socks

To wear with trainers (sneakers).

Follow any of the 3 sock recipes with the following changes:

Only work approximate 1.5cm (⅝in) of rib. The most suitable ribs to use are either 1 x 1 rib or picot edge (see Sock elements: Cuffs).

Omit the leg section completely.

For example: For the cuff-down or two-needle sock, you would cast on as given in the recipe and work the rib cuff for 1.5cm (⅝in) then jump straight to the heel or foot and continue with the rest of your sock as per the recipe.

For the toe-up sock, after working the heel, you would jump straight to the rib cuff, working approximately 1.5cm (⅝in) of rib before casting (binding) off.

No-heel socks

If you want to try a really simple sock in the round, with no heel, you could try this version of a 'no-heel sock' which has all the elements of a regular sock but without the heel. A travelling rib creates a twisting rib pattern that will cling to your foot without feeling loose or baggy.

You can follow either the cuff-down or toe-up sock recipe.

Cast on and work either the cuff or toe as given in the recipe.

Change to the following pattern for the leg:

*Rib round: (K3, p1) to the end of the round.

Repeat Rib round for a further 5 rounds and on the last of these 5 rounds, do not work the last p1.

Move your stitch marker to mark the new start of the round.*

Repeat from * to * for as many rounds as required, depending on the length you would like your sock to be.

Complete your sock by working the toe, or cuff, depending on which recipe you are following.

For the second sock, you can either work it the same as the first, or if preferred you can twist the rib in the opposite direction by working the repeat as follows:

**Rib round: (K3, p1) to the end of the round.

Repeat Rib round for a further 5 rounds. Knit 1 st and move your stitch marker to mark the new start of the round.**

Repeat from ** to ** for as many rounds as required, depending on the length you would like your sock to be.

Complete your sock by working the toe, or cuff, depending on which recipe you are following.

SOCK ELEMENTS

After working through the basic sock recipes, you may wish to try a few different cuffs, heels and toes. This section provides a selection of alternative options so that you can mix and match with the different elements of the recipes, to create your very own personalized socks. You may find that you prefer a 1 x 1 rib or a forethought heel or a rounded toe, but whichever you choose you'll have lots of knitting fun while you try them all out.

CUFFS

A cuff will either be the first thing you knit after casting on when working cuff-down, or the last thing you knit before casting (binding) off a toe-up sock. While there are many varieties of knitted cuff, they almost always serve the same purpose: to hold up the sock so that it fits around the leg and doesn't fall down, but not too tightly that it cuts into the leg and feels uncomfortable.

A cuff can also be a decorative feature, worked in a different colour to the main sock, or form part of the main sock pattern itself; cable designs or stripes can often blend seamlessly into the cuff and look really smart and stylish.

It's worth taking time to practise different types of cuff, because it goes without saying that we're all different, and so we will therefore have our own notion of the perfect cuff.

Also critical to achieving a comfortable cuff is your cast on/cast (bind) off method (see Sock techniques: Casting on, and Casting (binding) off), as this can make a huge difference to the wearability of your sock. You will always need to use a stretchy method, otherwise your cuff may not stretch over the widest part of your foot, or it could feel tight and uncomfortable around your leg. This can be particularly problematic with a toe-up sock, therefore trying different cuffs along with different cast on/cast (bind) off methods may also be a worthwhile exercise.

Here are a few different styles for you to try for your cuffs. All of these can be used with the cuff-down or toe-up sock recipes, and can even be adapted for most sizes of the two-needle sock recipe.

1 x 1 rib cuff

For a multiple of 2 stitches.

A simple and basic rib that alternates between 1 knit stitch and 1 purl stitch.

This stitch pattern is made up of 1 round only so it's easy to remember and creates neat, thin columns.

Rib round: (K1, p1) to the end.

Work the Rib round until you have reached the desired cuff length.

For cuff-down: Continue with rest of sock as given in your sock pattern.

For toe-up: You will now be ready to cast (bind) off.

For two-needle: Can be used if you have an odd number of sts (to account for the seam st).

Work in a 2-row pattern as follows:

Rib row 1 (RS): (K1, p1) to last st, k1.

Rib row 2: (P1, k1) to last st, p1.

Work the Rib rows 1-2 until you have reached the desired cuff length and continue rest of sock worked flat.

2 x 2 rib cuff

For a multiple of 4 stitches.

A simple rib that alternates between 2 knit stitches and 2 purl stitches.

As with a 1 x 1 rib, this stitch pattern is made up of 1 round only so it's easy to remember and creates neat columns. It is very stretchy and grips the leg well and bounces back into shape nicely.

Rib round: (K2, p2) to the end.

Work the Rib round until you have reached the desired cuff length.

For cuff-down: Continue with rest of sock as given in your sock pattern.

For toe-up: You will now be ready to cast (bind) off.

For two-needle: Can be used if you have a multiple of 4 sts plus 1 st (to account for the seam st); for example, use any of the sizes casting on 45 [49] [53] [57] sts.

Work in a 2-row pattern as follows:

Rib row 1 (RS): (K2, p2) to last st, k1.

Rib row 2: P1, (k2, p2) to the end.

Work the Rib rows 1-2 until you have reached the desired cuff length and continue rest of sock worked flat.

3 x 1 rib cuff

For a multiple of 4 stitches.

A simple rib that alternates between 3 knit stitches and 1 purl stitch.

As with a 1 x 1 rib, this stitch pattern is made up of 1 round only so it's easy to remember and creates wider, flat colums. It is stretchy and still grips the leg well.

Rib round: (K3, p1) to the end.

Work the Rib round until you have reached the desired cuff length.

For cuff-down: Continue with rest of sock as given in your sock pattern.

For toe-up: You will now be ready to cast (bind) off.

For two-needle: Can be used if you have a multiple of 4 sts plus 1 st (to account for the seam st); for example, use any of the sizes casting on 45 [49] [53] [57] sts.

Work in a 2-row pattern as follows:

Rib row 1 (RS): (K3, p1) to last st, k1.

Rib row 2: P1, (k1, p3) to the end.

Work the Rib rows 1-2 until you have reached the desired cuff length and continue rest of sock worked flat.

Half-twisted rib cuff

This is a variation on any rib where the knit stitches are all worked into the back leg (see Sock techniques: Basic stitches – K1tbl). This twists the stitch and creates an interesting texture and gives a stronger stitch definition that makes the knit stitches stand out like ridges. The purl stitches are worked as usual.

You can change any rib stitch to a half-twisted rib. I have used a 1 x 1 rib pattern to demonstrate, for a multiple of 2 stitches.

Rib round: (K1tbl, p1) to the end.

Work the Rib round until you have reached the desired cuff length.

For cuff-down: Continue with rest of sock as given in your sock pattern.

For toe-up: You will now be ready to cast (bind) off.

For two-needle: Can be used if you have an odd number of sts (to account for the seam st). Note that when you are working flat, you work the knit stitches twisted on the right side, and the purl stitches twisted on the wrong side.

Work in a 2-row pattern as follows:

Rib row 1 (RS): (K1tbl, p1) to last st, k1tbl.

Rib row 2: P1tbl, (k1, p1tbl) to the end.

Work the Rib rows 1-2 until you have reached the desired cuff length and continue rest of sock worked flat.

Two-colour rib cuff (corrugated rib cuff)

For a multiple of 2 or 4 stitches. I have used a (k2, p2) rib for a multiple of 4 stitches.

A rib that alternates between knit and purl sts and between colours. The knit sts are always worked in one colour and the purl sts in a different colour. When working, strand yarns across the wrong side (see Sock techniques: Working with more than one yarn/colour).

This highly decorative rib looks visually striking and adds a splash of colour to your socks. However, it is not as stretchy as other ribs due to the stranding. You can overcome this by using a slightly larger needle size for the cuff only.

Rib round: [With yarns at back, k2 in Yarn A, bring Yarn B to front, p2 in Yarn B, take Yarn B to back] to the end.

Work the Rib round until you have reached the desired cuff length.

For cuff-down: Continue with rest of sock as given in your sock pattern.

For toe-up: You will now be ready to cast (bind) off.

For two-needle: Can be used if you have a multiple of 4 sts plus 1 st (to account for the seam st). Work in a 2-row pattern as follows:

Rib row 1 (RS): [With yarns at back, k2 in Yarn A, bring Yarn B to front, p2 in Yarn B, take Yarn B to back] to last st, k1 in Yarn A.

Rib row 2: With yarns at front, p1 in Yarn A, [take Yarn B to back, k2 in Yarn B, bring Yarn B to front, p2 in Yarn A] to the end.

Work the Rib rows 1-2 until you have reached the desired cuff length and continue rest of sock worked flat.

Picot edge cuff

For a multiple of 2 stitches.

A folded cuff with an eyelet row that creates a picot edge. The hem is sewn to the inside when the sock is finished.

> *When sewing the slip stitch hem, maintain your tension/gauge so that you don't make the cuff feel tight.*

For cuff-down: Cast on your chosen number of stitches. Work a total of 10 rounds in stocking (stockinette) stitch.

Fold (eyelet) round: (K2tog, yo) to end.

Work in stocking (stockinette) stitch for a further 10 rounds, then continue with rest of sock as given in your pattern. When sock is complete, fold the eyelet round to the inside and sew in slip stitch to keep the hem edge in place.

For toe-up: Work a total of 10 rounds in stocking (stockinette) stitch, then work the Fold (eyelet) round as for cuff-down. Work for a further 10 rounds of stocking (stockinette) stitch. Cast (bind) off using a stretchy method, then fold the eyelet round to the inside and sew in slip stitch to keep the hem edge in place.

For two-needle: Can be used with an odd number of sts (to account for the seam st). After casting on, work flat in stocking (stockinette) stitch for 10 rows.

Fold (eyelet) row (RS): (K2tog, yo) to last stitch, k1.

Starting with a purl (WS) row, work for a further 9 rows of stocking (stockinette) stitch and continue with rest of sock as given in your pattern. When your sock is complete and seams are sewn, fold the eyelet row to the inside and sew in slip stitch to keep the hem edge in place.

HEELS

Heels come in all shapes and sizes. Some heels are square and some are rectangular; some are knitted along with the main sock, whereas others are knitted after the sock is complete. Some will suit only a cuff-down sock, and others a toe-up sock and there are heels that can be used with either method.

The possibilities are endless – you can mix and match all of the elements to create your own perfect sock and can use the heels to make a bold statement, by knitting them in a contrast yarn, or you can make your socks seamless by using the same yarn throughout.

But don't worry, because despite appearances, you don't need any special powers to work a sock heel, just your yarn and needles and a few handy tips.

Once you've mastered the techniques you'll be in a good position to be able to substitute a different sock heel to the one in your pattern, if you prefer.

Remember that if you have any little holes or gaps where you started your heel then you can use matching yarn to close these up at the end (see Sock techniques: Finishing your project – Fixing holes).

Cuff-down heel flap and gusset options

A heel flap and gusset creates a wide, shaped instep so there is plenty of room and, more importantly, it forms a similar shape to your foot and is really comfortable. The short row heel turn curves around the base of the heel for a really good fit.

The construction follows a few steps:

- First you work your chosen heel flap on exactly half of your stitches. This will create a rectangular piece of knitting.

- Next you work a few short rows to turn the heel (which is much easier than it sounds).

- Then you pick up stitches along the sides of the heel flap.

- Finally, you work in the round again over the whole sock, decreasing on each side of the instep to create a gusset, until you are back to your original number of sock stitches.

Note that:

- Regardless of what needles you are using for your main sock, 2 DPNs are the best needles to use for the heel (to work in rows).

- When you start the gusset you will use 3 stitch markers in total: the start of the round stitch marker; stitch marker 1; stitch marker 2. It is helpful to use a different coloured stitch marker to mark the start of the round and it can also be helpful to pop your stitch marker into a stitch rather than in between the stitches, so that it doesn't fall off the ends of the needles. Alternatively you can manoeuvre your stitches around, so that the stitch markers are not sitting on the ends of your needles.

COMMON HEEL (STOCKING (STOCKINETTE) STITCH WITH GARTER STITCH EDGE)

Sometimes called a gusset heel or a common heel flap and gusset.

Step 1: Setting up the heel

When you have completed your cuff and leg, as given in your pattern, you will finish at the end of the round, at the centre back of your knitting.

Remove the start of the round stitch marker.

Now work in rows using 2 DPNs.

Set-up row 1 (RS): K14 [15] [16] [17] [18], turn.

Set-up row 2: K3, p22 [24] [26] [28] [30], k3, turn.

Now you have half of your stitches on 1 DPN for the heel.

You will continue to work forward and back in rows on these 28 [30] [32] [34] [36] sts only for the heel flap, using 2 DPNs to knit in rows.

The remaining stitches not being worked are called the instep (top of foot) stitches. Leave these remaining stitches on your original needle(s) and ignore them while you work the heel.

Step 2: Knitting the heel flap

Heel row 1 (RS): Knit all sts.

Heel row 2: K3, purl to last 2 sts, k3.

Repeat Heel rows 1-2 for a further 10 [11] [12] [13] [14] times. You now have a rectangle with 11 [12] [13] [14] [15] garter stitch ridges along each side edge.

Step 3: Shaping (or turning) the heel

You will now shape the heel to create a small 'wedge' or 'pocket' of knitting. This is also called 'turning the heel' and is made by only working partway across each row before decreasing and turning, as follows:

Row 1 (RS): Slip 1 st *knitwise*, k15 [16] [17] [18] [19], skpo, k1, turn.

Row 2: Slip 1 st *purlwise*, p5, p2tog, p1, turn.

Note: There is a visible gap between the stitches already knitted and the stitches waiting to be worked; use this as a marker for the following rows.

Row 3: Slip 1 st *knitwise*, knit to 1 st before the gap, skpo, k1, turn.

Row 4: Slip 1 st *purlwise*, purl to 1 st before the gap, p2tog, p1, turn.

Repeat Rows 3-4 until all sts have been used up and 16 [18] [18] [20] [20] sts remain.

Note: On the last 2 rows for sizes XS [M] [XL] you will miss off the k1 or p1 at the end of each row, so for these sizes, the last 2 rows will read:

Second to last row (RS): Slip 1 st *knitwise*, knit to 1 st before the gap, skpo, turn.

Last row: Slip 1 st *purlwise*, purl to 1 st before the gap, p2tog, turn.

Your yarn is now situated at the right-hand side of the remaining heel stitches.

Step 4: Picking up the gusset stitches

Now you will connect the heel to the instep stitches, by picking up stitches along each side of the heel flap and knitting across the instep sts. You will have a lot more stitches than you started with originally, but in Step 5 you will decrease these extra stitches on each side of the instep to shape the gusset.

With RS of work facing, knit across the remaining 16 [18] [18] [20] [20] heel sts, with next DPN pick up and knit 12 [13] [14] [15] [16] sts along the first edge of the heel flap by inserting the tip of the right-hand needle in between each garter stitch ridge and inserting your needle under 2 loops of the edge yarn (this avoids making a loose stitch with visible holes) (see Sock techniques: Picking up stitches).

The general rule is to pick up 1 st before the first garter stitch ridge, 1 st in between every garter stitch ridge along the heel edge and 1 st after the last garter stitch ridge.

Note: *The number of sts picked up could vary if you have worked more (or less) heel rows and it's OK here to have a slightly different number of sts, but it would help to make a note of how many sts you picked up so that you can do the same along the opposite edge and also on the second sock.*

When you reach the end of the heel flap you will see a visible gap between the stitch just picked up and the instep sts.

To close this gap, pick up an extra stitch before the instep sts by working M1R (see Sock techniques: Increasing). It helps to use the next DPN to do this (so that stitch marker 1 will be between stitches and not at the end of a needle).

Place stitch marker 1, knit next 28 [30] [32] [34] [36] instep sts, place stitch marker 2, pick up and knit 1 st from gap before the heel flap by working M1L (see Sock techniques: Increasing).

Finally, with next DPN, pick up and knit 12 [13] [14] [15] [16] sts along the next edge of the heel flap as before.

Try to make sure that you pick up the same number of sts along this edge, so that both sides of the heel match.

You now have 70 [76] [80] [86] [90] sts and have reached the end of the round.

Remember, if you picked up more stitches than stated, then your stitch count may differ.

You can now switch back to your original type of needles (if you are not using DPNs for your main sock knitting).

Place another stitch marker to mark the new start of the round. This is the start of the round marker and is not numbered.

Note: *The start of the round position has now changed to sit on one side of the heel. This is now the best place to start each round because if you work in stripes or colourwork then you will need to carry yarn along the inside of your sock at this point. If the start of the round sat on the underside of your foot then you would feel the strands of yarn from the colour changes and this would be uncomfortable on the sole of your foot. However, it's worth noting that sock patterns do vary and some designers keep the start of the round in line with the centre point of the heel.*

Step 5: Shaping the gusset

Round 1: Knit to 3 sts before stitch marker 1, k2tog, k1, slip marker, k28 [30] [32] [34] [36] sts across to stitch marker 2, slip marker, k1, skpo, knit to end of round.

Note that your decreases should point to the sole of your foot.

Round 2: Knit all sts and slip markers.

Repeat Rounds 1-2 until 56 [60] [64] [68] [72] sts remain, ending after a Round 1. These will be the same number of stitches as you originally had for your leg, before starting the heel.

In addition to the start of the round marker, keep stitch markers 1 and 2 in place as you continue to knit your sock as per your pattern, moving them up every few rounds. You will need them to mark the toe shaping, later.

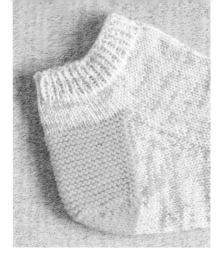

SLIPSTITCH HEEL

This is an alternative to the Common heel and is worked in exactly the same way overall, but instead of working your heel flap in stocking (stockinette) stitch, you will work in a slipstitch pattern. This is the heel also used in the cuff-down sock recipe (see Sock recipes).

Follow all of **Step 1** as for the Common heel then work Step 2 as follows:

Step 2: Knitting the heel flap

Heel row 1 (RS): Slip the first st *knitwise*, k1, *slip the next st *purlwise* (keeping yarn at back), k1; repeat from * to end of heel sts, turn.

Heel row 2: Slip the first st *purlwise* (with yarn at front), then purl every st to end of heel sts, turn.

Repeat Heel rows 1-2 for a further 12 [13] [14] [15] [16] times.

You now have a rectangle heel flap with 13 [14] [15] [16] [17] slipped sts along each side edge.

These edge stitches will appear slightly elongated and should be easy to count. You will use them later when picking up the gusset stitches.

To turn the heel: Follow **Step 3** of the Common heel.

To pick up the gusset stitches: Follow **Step 4** of the Common heel, with the only difference being that you pick up and knit 13 [14] [15] [16] [17] sts along each side of the heel.

To shape the gusset: Follow **Step 5** of the Common heel.

GARTER STITCH HEEL

This is another alternative to the Common heel and is worked in exactly the same way overall, but the heel flap is worked in garter stitch. This provides a thicker, double fabric which in turn is stronger and more durable.

Step 1: Setting up the heel

When you have completed your cuff and leg, as given in your pattern, you will finish at the end of the round, at the centre back of your knitting.

Remove the start of the round stitch marker.

Change to using two 2.25mm (US1) DPNs (or 1 needle size down from your main sock needles) and work in rows.

Set-up row 1 (RS): K14 [15] [16] [17] [18], turn.

Set-up row 2: K28 [30] [32] [34] [36], turn.

Now you have half of your stitches on 1 DPN for the heel.

You will continue to work forward and back in rows on these 28 [30] [32] [34] [36] sts only for the heel flap.

The remaining stitches not being worked are called the instep (top of foot) stitches. Leave these remaining stitches on your original needle(s) and ignore them while you work the heel.

Step 2: Knitting the heel flap

Heel row 1 (RS): K28 [30] [32] [34] [36], turn.

Heel row 2: K28 [30] [32] [34] [36], turn.

Repeat Heel rows 1-2 for a further 13 [14] [15] [16] [17] times.

You now have a heel flap with 14 [15] [16] [17] [18] garter stitch ridges along each side edge.

To turn the heel: Change back to your main sock needle sizes and follow **Step 3** of the Common heel.

To pick up the gusset stitches: Follow **Step 4** of the Common heel, with the only difference being that you pick up and knit 15 [16] [17] [18] [19] sts along each side of the heel.

To shape the gusset: Follow **Step 5** of the Common heel.

SOCK ELEMENTS

STRIPED (TWO-COLOUR) HEEL

This is our third alternative to the Common heel and is worked in a similar way, but without the garter stitch edge and it uses 2 colours, Yarn A and Yarn B.

Stranding the yarns across the back of stitches helps to make a thicker heel that is durable as well as being visually striking and colourful.

Step 1: Setting up the heel

When you have completed your cuff and leg, as given in your pattern, you will finish at the end of the round, at the centre back of your knitting.

Remove the start of the round stitch marker. Continue in current yarn colour (we will now call this Yarn A).

Row 1 (RS): K14 [15] [16] [17] [18], M1R, turn.

Note that an extra stitch has been made, because you need an odd number of stitches for this heel flap.

Use a spare DPN to work Row 2. Join in Yarn B.

Row 2: (P1 Yarn B, p1 Yarn A) 14 [15] [16] [17] [18] times, p1 Yarn B, turn.

You will now work back and forth in rows on these 29 [31] [33] [35] [37] sts only for the heel, using 2 DPNs. Slip remaining sts onto another DPN or a stitch holder. These stitches are the instep (top of foot) stitches. Ignore these stitches while you work the heel.

Step 2: Knitting the heel flap

Heel row 1: (K1 Yarn B, k1 Yarn A) to last st, k1 Yarn B, turn.

Heel row 2: (P1 Yarn B, p1 Yarn A) to last st, p1 Yarn B, turn.

Repeat Heel rows 1-2 for a further 5 [7] [7] [9] [9] times, then repeat Heel row 1 once more.

Next row (WS): With Yarn A, p2tog, purl to end, turn. (28 [30] [32] [34] [36] heel sts)

Continue with Yarn A.

To turn the heel: Follow **Step 3** of the Common heel.

To pick up the gusset stitches: Follow **Step 4** of the Common heel, with the only difference being that you pick up and knit 13 [14] [15] [16] [17] sts along each side of the heel.

To shape the gusset: Follow **Step 5** of the Common heel.

Toe-up options

SIMPLE SHAPED HEEL

A square heel, worked in 2 halves that can also be used for a cuff-down sock.

This heel is best worked with 2 DPNs.

You will start the heel at the point indicated in the pattern, working in rows over the first half of your stitches for the heel, which is 28 [30] [32] [34] [36] sts.

Slip the next 28 [30] [32] [34] [36] sts onto 1 DPN and leave the other stitches on your original needle(s). These other stitches are the instep (top of foot) stitches, but you will ignore them while you work the heel.

Work on the heel stitches only.

Row 1 (RS): Slip the first stitch then knit to the last 3 heel sts, k2tog, k1, turn.

Row 2: Slip the first stitch then purl to the last 3 sts, p2tog, p1, turn.

Repeat Rows 1-2 until 8 [10] [10] [12] [12] sts remain.

For the second half of the heel pick up each slipped stitch from the beginning of the previous rows (see Sock techniques: Picking up stitches), as follows:

Row 1 (RS): Slip the first stitch then knit to the end, pick up and knit the slipped stitch from next row of first half, turn.

Row 2: Slip the first stitch then purl to the end, pick up and purl the next slipped stitch from first half, turn.

Repeat these 2 rows until you have the same amount of stitches on your needle as you had originally.

Begin to knit sock in the round again, following your pattern instructions.

DOUBLE STITCH SHORT ROW HEEL (BOOMERANG HEEL)

A square heel, worked in 2 halves, can also be used for a cuff-down sock. Each half of the heel is worked using double stitch short rows (see Sock techniques: Short rows). 'Boomerang rounds' are worked in between to eliminate any holes in your heel edges.

> *If you knit your heel in a contrast colour the boomerang rounds will also be in the contrast colour.*

You will start the heel at the point indicated in the pattern, working in rows over the first half of your sts for the heel, which is 28 [30] [32] [34] [36] sts. It's easier if you switch to 2 DPNs to do this.

Leave the other half of your stitches on your original needle(s). These are the instep (top of foot) stitches, but you will ignore them while you work the heel.

Step 1: First half of heel

Row 1 (RS): K28 [30] [32] [34] [36] sts, turn and continue on these sts only.

Row 2: MDS (make double stitch) as follows: Slip 1 st *purlwise* with yarn in front. Pull yarn upwards, over needle and to the back to pull on the slipped st until it shows 2 legs of the st (and therefore looks like 2 sts), then bring yarn to front between needles and purl to end, turn.

Row 3: MDS, knit to DS, turn.

Row 4: MDS, bring yarn to front between needles and purl to DS, turn.

Repeat Rows 3-4 until 8 [10] [10] [10] [12] sts remain unworked in the middle between the DS sts, with 10 [10] [11] [12] [12] DS sts on each side of the heel.

Next, place a marker, knit across the unworked sts then knit all of the DS sts on first edge of heel (knitting both legs of the st – just as you would knit 2 sts together). You are now at the end of the heel sts.

Step 2: Boomerang rounds

Next round (first boomerang): Knit all sts in the round and when you reach the DS sts on the opposite edge of the heel, knit these DS sts as before through both legs of the DS. You will end at the marker.

Next round (second boomerang): Slip marker, knit to end and remove marker when you reach it.

Step 3: Second half of heel

Set-up row (RS): K9 [11] [11] [11] [13], turn.

Row 1: MDS, p9 [11] [11] [11] [13], turn.

Row 2: MDS, knit to DS, knit the DS and knit the next st after it, turn.

Row 3: MDS, purl to DS, purl the DS and purl the next st after it, turn.

Repeat Rows 2-3 until all the DS sts along the heel edges have been worked. You will end after a Row 2, at the end of the heel sts. Your heel is now complete.

Begin to knit sock in the round again, following your pattern instructions. There will be 1 final DS to knit at the start of the heel. Knit this DS as before when you reach it.

WRAP AND TURN SHORT ROW HEEL

A square heel, worked in 2 halves, can also be used for a cuff-down sock. This heel is best worked with 2 DPNs.

This is the heel used in the toe-up sock recipe (see Sock recipes), where there is a step-by-step photo guide.

You will start the heel at the point indicated in the pattern, working in rows over the first half of your stitches for the heel, which is 28 [30] [32] [34] [36] sts. It's easier if you switch to 2 DPNs to do this.

Slip the next 28 [30] [32] [34] [36] sts onto 1 DPN and leave the other half of your stitches on your original needle(s). These stitches are called the instep (top of foot) stitches, but you will ignore these stitches while you work the heel.

See Sock techniques: Short rows if you need a refresher.

Step 1: First half of heel

Row 1 (RS): Knit to last st, *bring yarn to front between needles, slip next st *purlwise* to right-hand needle, take yarn back between needles, slip st back to left-hand needle (RS W&T complete), turn*.

Row 2: Purl to last st, **take yarn to back between needles, slip last stitch *purlwise* to right-hand needle, bring yarn to front between needles, slip stitch back to left-hand needle (WS W&T complete), turn**.

Row 3: Knit to 1 st before the last wrapped st of the heel, work as from * to * to complete a RS W&T.

Row 4: Purl to 1 st before the last wrapped st of the heel, work as from ** to ** to complete a WS W&T.

Repeat Rows 3-4 until 8 [10] [10] [10] [12] sts remain unworked in the middle of the heel, between the wrapped stitches. The first half of the heel is now complete and there are 10 [10] [11] [12] [12] wrapped stitches on each side of the unworked stitches.

Step 2: Second half of heel

Some of your stitches will end up with a double wrap (2 stitches around the base of the stitch) and this really helps to keep the heel seam nice and neat, and without looking loose or holey.

Row 1 (RS): Knit to first wrapped st, pick up wrapped st and knit it together with st on needle, W&T the next st (this st now has 2 wraps).

Row 2: Purl to first wrapped st, pick up wrapped st and purl it together with st on needle, W&T the next st (this st now has 2 wraps).

Row 3: Knit to st with double wrap. Pick up both wraps and knit them together with st on needle, W&T the next st.

Row 4: Purl to st with double wrap. Pick up both wraps and purl them together with st on needle, W&T the next st.

Repeat Rows 3-4 until there is 1 double wrap left on each side of heel.

Next row: Repeat Row 3, working the last W&T on the next st from the instep.

Next row: Repeat Row 4, working the last W&T on the next st from the instep.

With RS now facing, begin to knit sock in the round again as per your pattern. When you come to the final wrapped sts on the instep (the ones just worked on last 2 rows), pick up these wraps and knit them together with their respective sts.

These last wraps can be quite tight so you may need to use a tapestry/ yarn needle to pick up the wraps.

TOE-UP GUSSET AND HEEL FLAP

As for the Cuff-down heel flap and gusset options, this heel creates a wide, shaped flap so there is plenty of room and comfort. Because you are working in a different direction, the gusset is formed first on the foot, using increases to create the triangular shape. Once the heel is turned on the centre heel stitches, the heel flap is formed as a rectangle while at the same time stitches from the gusset are decreased away at the end of each row – so there's no picking up of stitches required!

Step 1: Shaping the gusset

With the start of round marker at one side of the foot, place a second stitch marker at the halfway point of the round after the first 28 [30] [32] [34] [36] sts to mark the other side of the foot.

Round 1: Knit to marker, slip marker, k1, M1R, knit to last st of round, M1L, k1. (2 sts increased)

Round 2: Knit to end of round.

Repeat Rounds 1-2 until you have 56 [60] [64] [68] [72] sts on the sole. (84 [90] [96] [102] [108] total sts)

Step 2: Shaping (or turning) the heel

The heel turn is worked using double stitch short rows (see Sock techniques: Short rows).

You will now shape the heel to create a small 'wedge' or 'pocket' of knitting. This is also called 'turning the heel' and is made by only working partway across each row before decreasing and turning. Turn the work so your first row is a WS row and work the heel sts, as follows:

Row 1 (WS): P42 [45] [48] [51] [54], turn, leaving 14 [15] [16] [17] [18] gusset sts unworked.

Row 2: MDS, k27 [29] [31] [33] [35], turn, leaving 14 [15] [16] [17] [18] gusset sts unworked.

Row 3: MDS, purl to previous DS, turn.

Row 4: MDS, knit to previous DS, turn.

Rows 5-16: Repeat Rows 3-4 six times.

When working the next rows, remember when working the DS to work both legs together as if you are working a k2tog.

Row 17: MDS, purl to first DS, purl next 7 DS, p2tog (next DS and next plain st), turn, leaving 13 [14] [15] [16] [17] gusset sts unworked.

Row 18: Sl1 wyib, knit to first DS, knit next 7 DS, k2tog (next DS and next plain st), turn, leaving 13 [14] [15] [16] [17] gusset sts unworked.

Step 3: Knitting the heel flap

While the next rows will shape the rectangular heel flap, the gusset sts are slowly being incorporated and decreased away, which reattaches the heel stitches to the rest of the sock.

Row 1 (WS): Sl1 wyif, p26 [28] [30] [32] [34], p2tog, turn. (1 st decreased)

Row 2: Sl1 wyib, (k1, sl1 wyib) 13 [14] [15] [16] [17] times, ssk, turn. (1 st decreased)

Repeat Rows 1-2 until all gusset sts at each side are worked. Do not turn after final row.

Continue to work in the round on all 56 [60] [64] [68] [72] sts to work the leg of your sock.

Forethought heel

This heel can be used in toe-up or cuff-down socks. You add your heel after you have finished knitting the main body of the sock (the cuff, leg and toe). Although sometimes confused with an afterthought heel, planning the placement with waste yarn makes this a forethought heel (sometimes called a peasant heel).

It's the perfect option for self-striping yarn and colourwork socks because the number of stitches in the sock tube remains the same throughout, so any stripes or colourwork patterns will remain uninterrupted and look uniform from start to finish. However, there is no instep so it can be a slightly tighter fit than a more roomy heel flap and gusset.

This version is a square heel with banded decreases, sometimes called a classic wedge heel or a banded heel.

Step 1: Mark heel sts with waste yarn

At the point indicated in the pattern (or at the point that you want your heel to start) you will use a small length of waste yarn to mark the place where you would like your heel to be situated.

If you are unsure where to place the waste yarn to mark your heel postion while knitting, you can work a true afterthought heel instead. Once your tube is complete, try on your sock to determine the heel position and mark each end of 28 [30] [32] [34] [36] sts along this line with stitch markers. Then follow from Step 2 onwards to pick up sts above and below the line of marked sts, and once on the needles, you will need to carefully snip the sts open instead of removing the waste yarn.

Knit the next 28 [30] [32] [34] [36] sts with a contrasting piece of similar yarn (a smooth yarn works best as you will need to unpick this yarn later).

Slide these stitches back onto the left-hand needle, and work them again with working yarn, according to your pattern.

Complete your sock according to your pattern.

Step 2: Picking up stitches

With your sock tube off the needles and completely finished, you will now add the heel (see Sock techniques: Picking up stitches). This is best worked with a set of 5 DPNs.

Pick up the 28 [30] [32] [34] [36] sts from the round below the waste yarn by using the tip of the needle to lift the *right leg* of each stitch onto the first DPN.

Rotate the sock and pick up the 28 [30] [32] [34] [36] sts on the opposite side of the waste yarn in the same manner onto a second DPN. At this point you should have the same number of stitches as your main sock body.

Carefully remove the waste yarn sitting between the needles, first ensuring that all sts are secure on the needles. Have a couple of stitch markers handy in case you drop a st. You can place them onto a stitch marker until you're ready to knit.

Carefully divide your stitches onto 4 DPNs. You now have live stitches around a large opening, ready to knit your heel.

Step 3. Closing the gaps and knitting the heel

The start of the round is situated between the 2 DPNs on the underside of your heel.

Using your chosen yarn for the heel, begin working in the round as follows:

Round 1: Starting at second DPN, join in yarn and knit to end of needle, now there is a long gap before next DPN. Pick up 2 sts across the gap and place a stitch marker between these sts.

Knit all sts across next 2 DPNs, then pick up 2 sts across the next gap and place a stitch marker between these sts.

Knit across next DPN to end of round and mark start of round.

You now have 4 more sts than you started your sock with: 60 [64] [68] [72] [76] sts.

Round 2: Knit to 3 sts before first marker, k2tog, k1, slip marker, k1, skpo, knit to 3 sts before next marker, k2tog, k1, slip marker, k1, skpo, knit to end of round. (4 sts decreased)

Round 3: Knit to end.

Repeat the last 2 rounds until 20 [24] [24] [28] [28] sts remain.

Finally, knit across to the first marker only, so that your yarn is at the end of the needle ready to graft the sts together.

Step 4: Grafting the heel

Cut yarn, leaving a 30cm (12in) tail end.

Graft the heel closed using Kitchener stitch (see Sock techniques: Finishing your project).

TOES

Just like sock heels, there are lots of different styles and shapes of sock toes. These can range from long and pointy, to rounded or square in shape, but the good news is that sock toes are interchangeable, so if you find that a particular toe is more suited to the shape of your foot, then you can simply use this instead of the toe recommended in the pattern.

To help you work out which toe may be better for you, I have added some information for each toe about its shape. But you'll want to also try them on and see how they feel on your foot before deciding on your favourite.

I've given the instructions for these toes worked in the round for socks with 56 [60] [64] [68] [72] sts.

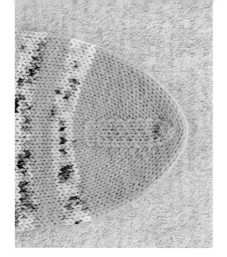

Toes for cuff-down socks

CLASSIC WEDGE TOE

A square shape toe.

When you have completed your foot, as given in your pattern, you will finish at the end of the round.

If you are using the cuff-down sock recipe (see Sock recipes) the end of the round is at the side of the heel. Remove the start of the round stitch marker and knit up to the next stitch marker left in place from the gusset decreasing. Use this as the new start of the round and it will line up your toes perfectly so that the decreases are at each side of the foot.

If you are using a different cuff-down pattern, make sure you start the round at one side of the foot, and place another marker at the halfway point on the other side of the foot to keep the toe symmetric.

Round 1: *K1, skpo, knit to 3 sts before next marker, k2tog, k1; repeat from * once more. (4 sts decreased)

Round 2: Knit all sts and slip markers.

Repeat Rounds 1-2 until 20 [24] [24] [28] [28] sts remain.

Join the toe stitches together using Kitchener Stitch (also called grafting) (see Sock techniques: Finishing your project). Then finish your sock as instructed in the pattern.

ROUNDED TOE

A rounded shape is achieved by decreasing evenly and gathering the final stitches, as you would decrease for the crown of a hat.

First you need to adjust the stitches for [S] [L] sizes only to work over a multiple of 8 as follows:

Next round for sizes [S] [L] only: (K [13] [15], k2tog) 4 times.

Continue for all sizes, which now have 56 [56] [64] [64] [72] sts, as follows:

Decrease round 1: (K6, k2tog) to the end. (49 [49] [56] [56] [63] sts)

Knit 6 rounds.

Decrease round 2: (K5, k2tog) to the end. (42 [42] [48] [48] [54] sts)

Knit 5 rounds.

Decrease round 3: (K4, k2tog) to the end. (35 [35] [40] [40] [45] sts)

Knit 4 rounds.

Decrease round 4: (K3, k2tog) to the end. (28 [28] [32] [32] [36] sts)

Knit 3 rounds.

Decrease round 5: (K2, k2tog) to the end. (21 [21] [24] [24] [27] sts)

Knit 2 rounds.

Decrease round 6: (K1, k2tog) to the end. (14 [14] [16] [16] [18] sts)

Knit 1 round.

Decrease round 7: (K2tog) to the end. (7 [7] [8] [8] [9] sts)

Cut yarn, leaving a long tail end and thread this onto a tapestry/yarn needle. Thread through the remaining sts and pull tightly to gather up the hole.

Secure the gathers with a few small stitches and weave in end on WS.

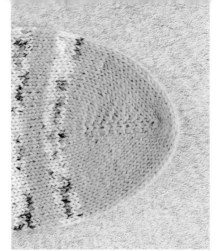

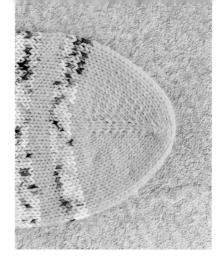

Toes for toe-up socks

FOUR-POINT TOE

A pointy toe finished with a small gather. Also sometimes called a star toe.

Divide your stitches into 4 and knit 1 round, placing stitch markers after knitting each section as follows:

Next round: (K14 [15] [16] [17] [18], place marker) 4 times.

Round 1: (Knit to 2 sts before marker, k2tog) to end. (4 sts decreased)

Round 2: Knit all sts and slip markers.

Repeat Rounds 1-2 until you have 8 sts remaining.

Cut yarn, leaving a long tail end and thread this end onto a tapestry/yarn needle. Thread through the remaining sts and pull tightly to gather up the hole. Secure the gathers with a few small stitches and weave in end on WS.

BASIC TOE

This toe is a rounded toe shape, and is the one used in the toe-up sock recipe (see Sock recipes) where there is also a step-by-step photo guide. Here we use stitch markers to indicate where the decreases are made, while the sock recipe is worked using magic loop over a long circular.

Using Judy's magic cast on method, cast on 20 [24] [24] [28] [28] sts over 2 DPNs – 10 [12] [12] [14] [14] sts on each needle (see Sock techniques: Casting on).

Place a marker at the start of the round and at the halfway point.

Work the increase shaping as follows:

Round 1: Knit all sts and slip markers.

Round 2: Kfb, knit to 1 st before the stitch marker, kfb, slip marker, kfb, knit to last st, kfb. (4 sts increased)

Round 3: Knit all sts and slip markers.

Repeat Rounds 2-3 until you have 56 [60] [64] [68] [72] sts in total.

Remember to tug the yarn before you knit the first stitch on each needle, so that you don't create little gaps or ladders along the sides of your socks.

Continue to work the leg of your sock as instructed in the pattern.

BANDED TOE

This toe is also rounded, but the different increase stitches form a neat line or 'band' along each side of the toe.

Work as given for Basic toe but replace Round 2 with the following:

Round 2: K1, M1L, knit to 1 st before the stitch marker, M1R, k1, slip marker, k1, M1L, knit to last st, M1R, k1. (4 sts increased)

Once the increases are complete, continue to work the leg of your sock as instructed in the pattern.

To create a deeper band along the side of the toe, you can work 2 stitches before and after the increases.

Work as given for Basic toe but replace Round 2 with the following:

Round 2: K2, M1L, knit to 2 sts before the stitch marker, M1R, k2, slip marker, k2, M1L, knit to last 2 sts, M1R, k2. (4 sts increased)

SOCK PROJECTS

Now the real fun begins as you move on to the next step, which is knitting socks from different patterns. I'm delighted to share these 10 exclusive sock designs with you, as there are so many different techniques to try, along with a fabulous selection of beautiful yarns and interesting stitch patterns. These 10 sock designers are really well known for their fantastic designs and attention to detail, and I hope you enjoy your creative journey as you build up your hand-knitted sock drawer and learn some new techniques along the way.

Due to tension/gauge and stitch patterns, the sizes differ from the sock recipes. Make sure to read the sizing information for your selected pattern to decide which size option will fit your foot best (see All about socks: Choosing the correct size).

Sloping Hills

BY WINWICK MUM

This is a great beginner project! Worked in a double knit (DK/8ply) yarn, these cuff-down socks work up quickly. The texture is made of all knits and purls, worked differently on right and left legs so your socks are mirrored.

You will need

Yarn

Baa Brighouse Baa Baa Brew; 100% British Bluefaced Leicester wool; 225m (244 yards) per 100g (3.5oz) skein

1 skein in Strangstry

This yarn is a DK (8ply) weight yarn, so any similar weight yarn would work well (see Checking your tension/gauge: Substituting yarn).

Needles

3.5mm (US4) needles for your preferred method of knitting in the round

If using a short circular needle, you will also need a set of DPNs in the same size for the cast on, heels and toes

4mm (US6) DPNs, optional for a looser cast on

Extras

Tape measure or ruler; stitch markers; stitch holder (optional); tapestry/yarn needle (for weaving in ends); sock blockers (optional), towel and wool wash for blocking (see Tools and materials: Extras)

Tension/Gauge

22 sts and 28 rows to 10 x 10cm (4 x 4in) measured in stocking (stockinette) stitch using 3.5mm (US4) needles

If you need to use a different needle size to achieve this tension/gauge, make sure that you use that needle size throughout (see Checking your tension/gauge).

Sizes

XS/S [M] [L] [XL] [2XL]

Knitted sock, actual knitted circumference:
18 [20] [22] [23.5] [25.5]cm (7 [7¾] [8½] [9¼] [10]in)

Will stretch to fit approximate foot circumference:
19 [21] [23] [24.5] [26.5]cm (7½ [8¼] [9] [9¾] [10½]in)

Construction

Cuff-down: these socks are cast on at the cuff and worked in the round to the heel. The **cuff** is a 2 x 2 rib and the **leg** is a textured pattern worked differently for right and left legs, worked from the charts or written instructions.

Heel flap & gusset: the heel is knitted on half of the stitches and worked in rows (to create a rectangular **heel flap**) in slipstitch (see Sock elements: Heels), then simple short rows are used to shape the **heel turn**. Stitches are picked up along each side of the heel flap and the **gusset** is worked in the round, decreasing at each side of the foot for the gusset shaping.

Foot: the **foot** continues the leg pattern on the instep and is worked in rounds.

Toe: the **toe** shaping uses simple gradual decreases as a slightly rounded variation to the classic wedge toe (see Sock elements: Toes) and then you will **graft** the toe seam using Kitchener stitch.

Project notes

This sock is worked in a thicker yarn, so there are fewer stitches to cast on. Make sure to check the sizing to determine which size will best fit your foot. Although our cuff-down recipe uses 4ply (fingering) yarn, the heel is the same construction as for these socks so you may find the step-by-step guide useful as a refresher if needed (see Sock recipes: Cuff-down socks).

Stitch patterns

Key
☐ knit
⊡ purl

Left pattern (14 sts)

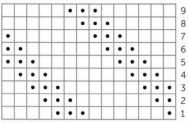

14 13 12 11 10 9 8 7 6 5 4 3 2 1

Pattern round 1: P1, k6, p3, k4.

Pattern round 2: P2, k6, p3, k3.

Pattern round 3: P3, k6, p3, k2.

Pattern round 4: K1, p3, k6, p3, k1.

Pattern round 5: K2, p3, k6, p3.

Pattern round 6: K3, p3, k6, p2.

Pattern round 7: K4, p3, k6, p1.

Pattern round 8: K5, p3, k6.

Pattern round 9: K6, p3, k5.

Right pattern (14 sts)

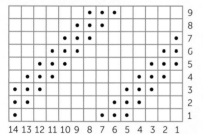

14 13 12 11 10 9 8 7 6 5 4 3 2 1

Pattern round 1: K4, p3, k6, p1.

Pattern round 2: K3, p3, k6, p2.

Pattern round 3: K2, p3, k6, p3.

Pattern round 4: K1, p3, k6, p3, k1.

Pattern round 5: P3, k6, p3, k2.

Pattern round 6: P2, k6, p3, k3.

Pattern round 7: P1, k6, p3, k4.

Pattern round 8: K6, p3, k5.

Pattern round 9: K5, p3, k6.

Instructions

Cuff

Cast on 40 [44] [48] [52] [56] sts onto 1 DPN. Use the larger DPN if you prefer a looser cuff.

For size XS/S: Rib round 1: *P1, k1, (p2, p2) 4 times, k1, p1; repeat from * once more.

For size M: Rib round 1: *K1, p1, (k2, p2) 4 times, k2, p1, k1; repeat from * once more.

For size L: Rib round 1: *K1, (p2, k2) 5 times, p2, k1; repeat from * once more.

For size XL: Rib round 1: *(K2, p2) 6 times, k2; repeat from * once more.

For size 2XL: Rib round 1: *P1, (k2, p2) 6 times, k2, p1; repeat from * once more.

All sizes: Do not turn your work (keep the RS of knitting facing you).

Next, starting from the opposite end of the DPN to the working yarn, carefully slip the stitches purlwise onto a short circular needle (or spread your stitches evenly over 4 DPNs), keeping RS of work facing at all times. Join to start knitting in the round (see Knitting in the round: Joining the round). Place a stitch marker in the first or last stitch of the round, moving it up as you work.

Rib rounds 2-12: Work as for Rib round 1 for your size.

Leg

Make sure to work either Left or Right pattern for the appropriate sock. You can work the pattern from the chart or written instructions.

For size XS/S: Round 1: *P1, k2, work Pattern round 1, k2, p1; repeat from * once more.

For size M: Round 1: *K1, p1, k2, work Pattern round 1, k2, p1, k1; repeat from * once more.

For size L: Round 1: *K1, p2, k2, work Pattern round 1, k2, p2, k1; repeat from * once more.

For size XL: Round 1: *K2, p2, k2, work Pattern round 1, k2, p2, k2; repeat from * once more.

For size 2XL: Round 1: *P1, k2, p2, k2, work Pattern round 1, k2, p2, k2, p1; repeat from * once more.

All sizes: Round 1 sets pattern and position of chart. Continue as set, and following correct row of chart, until leg measures 15cm (6in) or desired length of leg. Keep note of which pattern round you finish on to continue the pattern on the instep when working the foot later.

Round 2: Knit to marker, slip marker, knit in pattern across instep to next marker, slip marker, knit to end of round.

Repeat the last 2 rounds until 40 [44] [48] [52] [56] sts remain.

Foot

Continue working straight, maintaining pattern as set on instep sts and stocking (stockinette) stitch for the sole sts, until the sock measures approximately 3.5 [3.5] [4] [4] [5]cm (1¼ [1¼] [1½] [1½] [2]in) less than the desired foot length (see All about socks: Choosing the correct size).

Toe

If you are using a short circular needle, you will need to change to using DPNs when there are too few sts on the circular needle.

Next round (partial): Remove start of round marker, knit to next marker. This is the new start of round marker.

Round 1: *K1, ssk, knit to 3 sts before next marker, k2tog, k1; repeat from * once more. (4 sts decreased)

Rounds 2-3: Knit to end of round, slipping markers.

Rounds 4-6: Repeat Rounds 1-3 once more.

Round 7: Repeat Round 1.

Round 8: Knit to end of round, slipping markers.

Repeat Rounds 7-8 until 24 [28] [28] [32] [32] sts remain.

To finish

Divide sts over 2 DPNs and use Kitchener stitch to graft toes together. Weave in all ends and trim. Block your socks and leave to dry completely (see Sock techniques: Finishing your project).

Heel flap

Change to DPNs if you are using a short circular needle.

Row 1 (RS): K2, (sl1, k1) until you have 20 [22] [24] [26] [28] sts on your needle, turn. You can place the remaining sts on a stitch holder or spare needle while you work if you prefer.

Row 2: Sl1, purl to end, turn.

Row 3: (Sl1, k1) to end, turn.

Repeat Rows 2-3 until heel measures 4.5 [5] [5] [6.5] [7.5]cm (1¾ [2] [2] [2½] [3]in), ending after a Row 3.

Heel turn

Row 1 (WS): Sl1, p11 [12] [13] [14] [15], p2tog, p1, turn.

Row 2: Sl1, k5, ssk, k1, turn.

Row 3: Sl1, p6, p2tog, p1, turn.

Row 4: Sl1, k7, ssk, k1, turn.

Continue in this way, adding 1 stitch between slip stitch and decrease on each row (i.e. Row 5, Sl1, p8, p2tog, p1), until all of the heel sts are used. You may find that on the last 2 rows you don't need to work the final p1 or k1.

Gusset

With RS of heel flap facing you, knit across heel sts if required to bring you to the left-hand side of the heel sts.

Pick up and knit 1 st for each slipped st down the left-hand side of the heel flap (see Sock techniques: Picking up stitches), pick up and knit 1 st from the gap between the end of the picked up sts and the instep sts using M1R (see Sock techniques: Increasing), place stitch marker, work across the held instep sts in pattern as set, making sure to work the next pattern round after you stopped for the leg, place marker at end of instep sts, pick up and knit 1 st from the gap before the heel flap using M1L, then pick up and knit 1 st for each slipped st up the right-hand edge of the heel flap.

Place another stitch marker to mark the new start of the round. A stitch count is not given because this will vary from person to person, depending on how many rows you knitted for your heel.

Gusset shaping

Round 1: Knit to 3 sts before the marker, k2tog, k1, slip marker, knit in pattern across instep to next marker, slip marker, k1, ssk, knit to end of round. (2 sts decreased)

Under the Stars

BY EMMA POTTER

A very special pair of ankle socks made using 3 strands of super luxurious yarn held together. You'll want to try out all sorts of combinations for this classic cuff-down pair.

You will need

Yarn
3 types of yarn are used:

Yarn A: Miss Moffat Yarns 4ply sock yarn; 75% Merino superwash wool, 25% nylon; 400m (437 yards) per 100g (3.5oz) skein

1 skein in Golden Gate (Yarn A)

Yarn B: DROPS Brushed Alpaca Silk; 77% alpaca, 23% silk; 140m (153 yards) per 25g (0.88oz) ball

1 ball in Rust (Yarn B)

Yarn C: King Cole Cosmos; 76% glitter yarn, 24% payette; 393m (430 yards) per 25g (0.88oz) ball

1 ball in Copper (Yarn C)

Yarn A is a regular 4ply (fingering) weight yarn; Yarn B is a mix of alpaca and silk but any high-loft yarn such as alpaca or mohair could be used; Yarn C is a thin fashion/novelty yarn but a lace weight yarn could be used (see Checking your tension/gauge: Substituting yarn).

Needles
2.5mm (US2 or US1) needles for your preferred method of knitting in the round

If using a short circular needle, you will also need a set of DPNs in the same size for the cast on, heels and toes

Extras
Tape measure or ruler; stitch markers; stitch holder (optional); tapestry/yarn needle (for weaving in ends); sock blockers (optional), towel and wool wash for blocking (see Tools and materials: Extras)

Tension/Gauge
29 sts and 40 rows to 10 x 10cm (4 x 4in) measured in stocking (stockinette) stitch using 2.5mm (US2 or US1) needles

Since you will be mixing yarns, it is really important to measure your tension/gauge before you start. Use whatever size needle achieves the proper tension/gauge (see Checking you tension/gauge).

Sizes
XS [S] [M] [L] [XL]

Knitted sock, actual knitted circumference:
19 [20.5] [22] [23.5] [25]cm (7½ [8] [8¾] [9¼] [9¾]in)

Construction

Cuff-down: these socks are cast on at the cuff and worked in the round to the heel. The **cuff** is a 2 x 2 rib and the **leg** is ankle length in plain stocking (stockinette) stitch.

Heel flap & gusset: the heel is knitted on half of the stitches and worked in rows (to create a rectangular **heel flap**) in slipstitch (see Sock elements: Heels), then simple short rows are used to shape the **heel turn**. Stitches are picked up along each side of the heel flap and the **gusset** is worked in the round, decreasing at each side of the foot for the gusset shaping.

Foot: the **foot** is worked in stocking (stockinette) stitch.

Toe: the **toe** shaping uses simple gradual decreases as a slightly rounded variation to the classic wedge toe (see Sock elements: Toes) and then you will **graft** the toe seam using Kitchener stitch.

Project notes

Using more than 1 strand of yarn held together means that the fabric will be thicker, and these socks have a small amount of positive ease. They would work well for bed socks, so choose the size closest to your actual foot circumference (see All about socks: Choosing the correct size).

Instructions

Cuff

Holding Yarn A and Yarn B together (see Sock techniques: Working with more than one yarn/colour), loosely cast on 56 [60] [64] [68] [72] sts onto 1 DPN.

Rib round: (K2, p2) to the end. Do not turn your work (keep the RS of knitting facing you).

Next, starting from the opposite end of the DPN to the working yarn, carefully slip the stitches purlwise onto a short circular needle (or spread your stitches evenly over 4 DPNs), keeping RS of work facing at all times. Join to start knitting in the round (see Knitting in the round: Joining the round). Place a stitch marker in the first or last stitch of the round, moving it up as you work.

Continue in rib pattern (repeating Rib round) until you have completed 10 rounds in total or desired length.

Leg

Join in Yarn C.

Holding all 3 strands (Yarn A, Yarn B and Yarn C) together, work in stocking (stockinette) stitch (knit every round) throughout until sock measures 9cm (3½in) or desired length.

Heel flap

Drop Yarn C and work heel flap with Yarn A and Yarn B together.

Change to DPNs if you are using a short circular needle.

Row 1 (RS): (Sl1, k1) until you have 28 [30] [32] [34] [36] sts on your needle, turn.

You can place the remaining stitches on a stitch holder or spare needle while you work if you prefer.

Row 2: Sl1, purl to end, turn.

Row 3: (Sl1, k1) to end, turn.

Repeat Rows 2-3 a total of 10 [12] [12] [14] [16] times.

Heel turn

Row 1 (WS): Sl1, p14 [15] [16] [17] [18], p2tog, p1, turn.

Row 2: Sl1, k3, ssk, k1, turn.

Row 3: Sl1, purl to 1 st before gap, p2tog, p1, turn.

Row 4: Sl1, knit to 1 st before gap, k2tog, k1, turn.

Repeat Rows 3-4 until all heel sts have been worked. Depending on the number of sts you started with, you may need to end the final 2 rows with p2tog and k2tog. Do not turn after the final RS row. (16 [18] [18] [20] [20] heel sts)

Gusset

Continue with 2 strands held together, pick up and knit 10 [12] [12] [14] [16] sts along the edge of the heel flap, place stitch marker, knit across 28 [30] [32] [34] [36] instep sts, place marker, join Yarn C again and continue with 3 strands held together, pick up and knit 10 [12] [12] [14] [16] sts up the other edge of the heel flap. Place another stitch marker to mark the new start of the round. (64 [70] [74] [82] [88] sts)

Gusset shaping

Round 1: Knit to 3 sts before the marker, k2tog, k1, slip marker, knit instep sts, slip marker, k1, ssk, knit to end of round. (2 sts decreased)

Round 2: Knit to end of round.

Repeat these 2 rounds until you have 56 [60] [64] [68] [72] sts.

Foot

Continue holding all 3 strands (Yarn A, Yarn B and Yarn C) together, work in stocking (stockinette) stitch (knit every round) throughout until sock measures 3.5 [4] [4.5] [5]cm (1¼ [1½] [1¾] [2]in) less than the desired foot length (see All about socks: Choosing the correct size).

Toe

Drop Yarn C and work toe with Yarn A and Yarn B held together. If you are using a short circular needle, you will need to change to DPNs when there are too few sts on the circular needle.

Next round (partial): Remove start of round marker, knit to next marker. This is the new start of round marker.

Round 1: *K1, ssk, knit to 3 sts before next marker, k2tog, k1; repeat from * once more. (4 sts decreased)

Round 2: Knit to end of round, slipping markers.

Round 3: Knit to end of round, slipping markers.

Repeat Rounds 1-3 once more, then repeat Rounds 1-2 for a further 4 [5] [6] [6] [7] times, and repeat Round 1 once more. (24 [28] [28] [32] [32] sts)

To finish

Divide sts over 2 DPNs and use Kitchener stitch to graft toes together. Weave in all ends and trim. Block your socks and leave to dry completely (see Sock techniques: Finishing your project).

Twisting Pathways

BY VIKKI BIRD

These toe-up socks are a journey along a path through twisty eye-catching cables, a forethought heel, and ending back at home with cosy feet.

You will need

Yarn

Eden Cottage Yarns Tempo 4ply; 75% Merino superwash wool, 25% nylon; 400m (436 yards) per 100g (3.5oz) skein

1 skein in Misty Woods

This yarn is a 4ply (fingering) weight yarn, so any similar weight yarn would work well (see Checking your tension/gauge: Substituting yarn).

Needles

2.5mm (US2 or US1) needles for your preferred method of knitting in the round

If using a short circular needle, you will also need a set of DPNs in the same size for the toes and heels

Extras

2 cable needles; waste yarn; tape measure or ruler; 4 stitch markers; tapestry/yarn needle (for weaving in ends); sock blockers (optional), towel and wool wash for blocking (see Tools and materials: Extras)

Tension/Gauge

32 sts and 44 rows to 10 x 10cm (4 x 4in) measured in stocking (stockinette) stitch using 2.5mm (US2 or US1) needles

If you need to use a different needle size to achieve this tension/gauge, make sure that you use that needle size throughout (see Checking your tension/gauge).

Sizes

XS [S] [M/L] [XL/2XL] [3XL]

Knitted sock, actual knitted circumference:

16.5 [19] [21.5] [24] [26.5]cm (6¼ [8] [8¾] [9½] [10½]in)

Will stretch to fit approximate foot circumference:

17.5 [20] [22.5] [25] [27.5]cm (6¾ [8¼] [9] [9¾] [10¾]in)

Construction

Toe-up: these socks are cast on at the toe with a closed cast-on. The **toe** uses simple gradual increases as a slightly rounded variation to the classic wedge toe (see Sock elements: Toes) and the **foot** is worked with the sole in stocking (stockinette) stitch and the instep (top of foot) worked in the cable pattern, then heel position is marked with waste yarn.

Leg: the cable pattern is continued on the front of the **leg**, which can be made to your preferred length.

Cuff: the **cuff** is worked in 2 x 2 rib, then cast (bind) off using a stretchy cast (bind) off.

Forethought heel: the heel stitches are picked up from the waste yarn, then the **forethought heel** (see Sock elements: Heels) is worked in decreases in the round then **grafted** using Kitchener stitch.

Project notes

Because of the pattern repeat and tension/gauge, the sizes for these socks differ from the recipes so make sure to check the sizing before you begin (see All about socks: Choosing the correct size). Cables create a tighter tension due to the crossing over of stitches, therefore more stitches are needed compared with stocking stitch.

Special abbreviations

Cr8B, place next 5 stitches on cable needle, hold at back, k3 from left-hand needle, return 2 left-most sts from cable needle to left-hand needle, move cable needle to front, p2 from left-hand needle, k3 from cable needle

Cr8F, place next 3 stitches to first cable needle and hold at front, place next 2 stitches to second cable needle and hold at back, k3 from left-hand needle, p2 from back cable needle, k3 from front cable needle (see Sock techniques: Cables)

Stitch pattern

Cable pattern (over 32 sts)

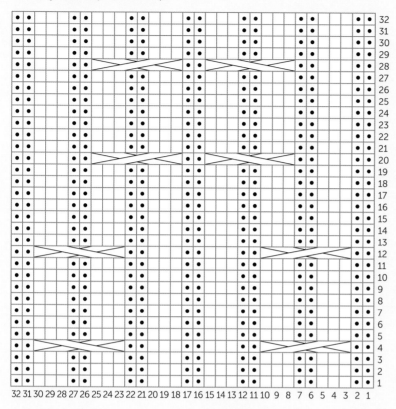

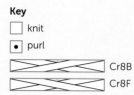

Key

☐ knit

• purl

▨▨ Cr8B

▨▨ Cr8F

Rounds 1-3: (P2, k3) 6 times, p2.

Round 4: P2, Cr8B, (p2, k3) twice, p2, Cr8F, p2.

Rounds 5-11: (P2, k3) 6 times, p2.

Round 12: P2, Cr8B, (p2, k3) twice, p2, Cr8F, p2.

Rounds 13-19: (P2, k3) 6 times, p2.

Round 20: P2, k3, p2, Cr8F, p2, Cr8B, p2, k3, p2.

Rounds 21-27: (P2, k3) 6 times, p2.

Round 28: P2, k3, p2, Cr8F, p2, Cr8B, p2, k3, p2.

Rounds 29-32: (P2, k3) 6 times, p2.

Instructions

Toe

With 2.5mm (US2 or US1) needles, cast on 8 sts using a closed cast on method such as Judy's magic cast on (see Sock techniques: Casting on, for an illustrated guide).

Set-up round: K4, place marker, k4, place marker for start of round. Move the markers up as you work.

Round 1: (K1, M1L, knit to last st before marker, M1R, k1) twice. (4 sts increased)

Repeat Round 1 another 4 [5] [6] [7] [8] times. (28 [32] [36] [40] [44] sts)

Round 2: Knit to end of round.

Round 3: (K1, M1L, knit to last st before marker, M1R, k1) twice. (4 sts increased)

Repeat Rounds 2-3 another 5 [6] [7] [8] [9] times. (52 [60] [68] [76] [84] sts)

Next round: Knit to end of round.

Foot

> *Make sure to use the correct set-up rounds for your size as follows:*

SIZE XS ONLY:

Set-up round: Knit to marker, slip marker, (p2, k1, M1L, k1) 6 times, p2. (58 sts)

Round 1: Knit to marker, slip marker, work Round 1 of Cable pattern from chart or written instructions to end of round.

SIZE S ONLY:

Set-up round: Knit to marker, slip marker, k2, place cable marker, (p2, k1, M1L, k1) 6 times, p2, place cable marker, k2. (66 sts)

Round 1: Knit to marker, slip marker, k2, slip marker, work Round 1 of Cable pattern from chart or written instructions, slip marker, k2.

SIZE M/L ONLY:

Set-up round: Knit to marker, slip marker, p2, k2, place cable marker, (p2, k1, M1L, k1) 6 times, p2, place cable marker, k2, p2. (74 sts)

Round 1: Knit to marker, slip marker, p2, k2, slip marker, work Round 1 of Cable pattern from chart or written instructions, slip marker, k2, p2.

SIZE XL/2XL ONLY:

Set-up round: Knit to marker, slip marker, k2, p2, k2, place cable marker, (p2, k1, M1L, k1) 6 times, p2, place cable marker, k2, p2, k2. (82 sts)

Round 1: Knit to marker, slip marker, k2, p2, k2, slip marker, work Round 1 of Cable pattern from chart or written instructions, slip marker, k2, p2, k2.

SIZE 3XL ONLY:

Set-up round: Knit to marker, slip marker, (p2, k2) twice, place cable marker, (p2, k1, M1L, k1) 6 times, p2, place cable marker, (k2, p2) twice. (90 sts)

Round 1: Knit to marker, slip marker, (p2, k2) twice, slip marker, work Round 1 of Cable pattern from chart or written instructions, slip marker, (k2, p2) twice.

ALL SIZES:

Round 1 sets stocking (stockinette) on sole (bottom of foot) and cable pattern on instep (top of foot).

Continue in patterns as set, repeating Rounds 1-30 of Cable pattern throughout, until sock measures 5 [6] [6.5] [7] [8]cm (2 [2¼] [2½] [2¾] [3] in) less than the desired foot length (see All about socks: Choosing the correct size).

Marking heel position

The next round sets the position of the heel, which will be worked once the rest of the sock is complete.

The waste yarn you use to mark the heel should be thinner than your chosen yarn in a smooth fibre like cotton. It is also useful to use a contrasting colour to be easily seen against the rest of the sock

Next round: Using waste yarn, k26 [30] [34] [38] [42] sts, then slip these sts back to left-hand needle. Using working yarn knit waste yarn sts to marker, slip marker, work in pattern to end of round as set.

Leg

Continue working in patterns as set until leg measures approximately 3 [3.5] [4] [4.5] [5]cm (1⅛ [1⅜] [1⅝] [1¾] [2]in) less than desired leg length, ending after a Round 8, 16, 24 or 32 of Cable pattern.

You can work the leg to be the same length as the foot. Fold the sock in half at the heel marker and check the length against what you have worked for the foot.

Cuff

Decrease and set rib as instructed for your size as follows:

SIZE XS ONLY:

Decrease round: (K2, p2) to 2 sts before marker, k2, remove marker, (p2, k2tog, k1) 3 times, (p2, k1, ssk) 3 times, p2. (52 sts)

Rib round: (K2, p2) to end of round.

SIZE S ONLY:

Decrease round: (P2, k2) to 2 sts before marker, p2, remove marker, k2, remove marker, (p2, k2tog, k1) 3 times, (p2, k1, ssk) 3 times, p2, remove marker, k2. (60 sts)

Rib round: (P2, k2) to end of round.

SIZE M/L ONLY:

Decrease round: (K2, p2) to 2 sts before marker, k2, remove marker, p2, k2, remove marker, (p2, k2tog, k1) 3 times, (p2, k1, ssk) 3 times, p2, remove marker, k2, p2. (68 sts)

Rib round: (K2, p2) to end of round.

SIZE XL/2XL ONLY:

Decrease round: (P2, k2) to 2 sts before marker, p2, remove marker, k2, p2, k2, remove marker, (p2, k2tog, k1) 3 times, (p2, k1, ssk) 3 times, p2, remove marker, k2, p2, k2. (76 sts)

Rib round: (P2, k2) to end of round.

SIZE 3XL ONLY:

Decrease round: (K2, p2) to 2 sts before marker, k2, remove marker, (p2, k2) twice, remove marker, (p2, k2tog, k1) 3 times, (p2, k1, ssk) 3 times, p2, remove marker, (k2, p2) twice. (84 sts)

Rib round: (K2, p2) to end of round.

ALL SIZES:

Continue in 2 x 2 rib as set in Rib round for a further 11 [13] [15] [17] [19] rounds.

Cast off all sts using a stretchy cast off, such as Jeny's surprisingly stretchy cast (bind) off (see Sock techniques: Casting (binding) off, for an illustrated guide).

Forethought heel

If you need a refresher on picking up stitches from the waste yarn, see Sock techniques: Picking up stitches.

Using your preferred needles, pick up 26 [30] [34] [38] [42] heel sts from the round below the waste yarn by using the tip of the needle to lift the right leg of each st onto the needle.

Rotate the sock and using a second DPN or needle tip, pick up 26 [30] [34] [38] [42] heel stitches from the round above the waste yarn in the same manner. (52 [60] [68] [76] [84] sts)

Carefully remove the waste yarn from between the 2 needles.

Set-up round: Join in yarn, pick up and knit 2 sts in the gap between the 2 needles, placing the start of round marker after the first st, then knit 26 [30] [34] [38] [42] sts from the bottom needle, pick up and knit 2 sts in the gap as before placing a side marker between these 2 sts, k26 [30] [34] [38] [42] sts from top needle, k1 (first picked up st from the gap) to join round. (56 [64] [72] [80] [88] sts)

Rounds 1-3: Knit to end of round.

Round 4: (K1, ssk, knit to 3 sts before marker, k2tog, k1, slip marker) twice. (4 sts decreased)

Round 5: Knit.

Repeat Rounds 4-5 another 8 [10] [11] [12] [14] times. (20 [20] [24] [28] [28] sts)

To finish

Divide sts over 2 DPNs and use Kitchener stitch to graft heel together. Weave in all ends and trim. Block your socks and leave to dry completely (see Sock techniques: Finishing your project).

Spring Lace

BY RACHEL FLETCHER

This design features a simple lace detail on the front of the leg and instep. Perfect with a speckled yarn or even a solid colour, these cuff-down socks use some classic sock elements with an extra twist.

You will need

Yarn

Birdstreet Yarn Hardy Sock; 100% Bluefaced Leicester superwash wool; 400m (437 yards) per 100g (3.5oz) skein

1 skein in Amnesia

This yarn is a 4ply (fingering) weight yarn, so any similar weight yarn would work well (see Checking your tension/gauge: Substituting yarn).

Needles

2.5mm (US2 or US1) needles for your preferred method of knitting in the round

If using a short circular needle, you will also need a set of DPNs in the same size for the cast on, heels and toes

Extras

Tape measure or ruler; stitch markers; stitch holder (optional); tapestry/yarn needle (for weaving in ends); sock blockers (optional), towel and wool wash for blocking (see Tools and materials: Extras)

Tension/Gauge

32 sts and 48 rows to 10 x 10cm (4 x 4in) measured in stocking (stockinette) stitch using 2.5mm (US2 or US1) needles

If you need to use a different needle size to achieve this tension/gauge, make sure that you use that needle size throughout (see Checking your tension/gauge).

Sizes

XS/S [M/L] [XL]

Knitted sock, actual knitted circumference:
17.5 [20] [22.5]cm (7 [7¾] [8¾]in)

Will stretch to fit approximate foot circumference:
18.5 [21] [23.5]cm (7¼ [8¼] [9¼]in)

Construction

Cuff-down: these socks are cast on at the cuff and worked in the round to the heel. The **cuff** is a 1 x 1 half-twisted rib and the front of the **leg** is a lace pattern while the back of the leg is in stocking (stockinette) stitch.

Heel flap & gusset: the heel is knitted on odd number of approximately half of the stitches, and worked in rows (to create a rectangular **heel flap**) in slipstitch (see Sock elements: Heels), then simple short rows are used to shape the **heel turn**. Stitches are picked up along each side of the heel flap and the **gusset** is worked in the round, decreasing at each side of the foot for the gusset shaping.

Foot: the **foot** is then worked in rounds with the lace pattern continued on the instep sts.

Toe: the **toe** shaping uses simple gradual decreases as a slightly rounded variation to the classic wedge toe (see Sock elements: Toes) and then you will **graft** the toe seam using Kitchener stitch.

Project notes

Make sure to check the pattern sizing to determine which size will best fit your foot. The heel flap is worked over an odd number of stitches so pay attention when instructed to turn for the heel. The heel and toes of the recipe for cuff-down socks are similar to the ones used in this sock, so you can use the step-by-step guides there for a refresher if needed (see Sock recipes: Cuff-down socks). Note that the stitch count varies over different rounds for the lace pattern due to the sl1, k2, psso in one round, and the k1, yo, k1 of the same stitches in the next round.

Stitch patterns

Lace pattern (size XS/S)

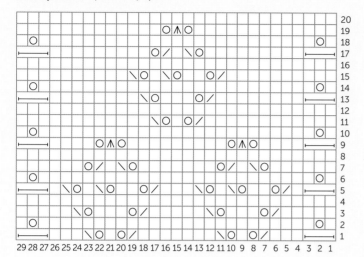

Round 1 (RS): Sl1, k2, psso, k3, k2tog, yo, k1, yo, ssk, k7, k2tog, yo, k1, yo, ssk, k3, sl1, k2, psso.

Rounds 2, 6, 10, 14 and 18: K1, yo, k25, yo, k1.

Round 3: K5, k2tog, yo, k3, yo, ssk, k5, k2tog, yo, k3, yo, ssk, k5.

Rounds 4, 8, 12 and 16: Knit.

Round 5: Sl1, k2, psso, k1, k2tog, yo, k2, yo, ssk, k1, yo, ssk, k3, k2tog, yo, k2, yo, ssk, k1, yo, ssk, k1, sl1, k2, psso.

Round 7: K6, yo, ssk, k1, k2tog, yo, k7, yo, ssk, k1, k2tog, yo, k6.

Round 9: Sl1, k2, psso, k4, yo, cdd, yo, k9, yo, cdd, yo, k4, sl1, k2, psso.

Round 11: K12, k2tog, yo, k1, yo, ssk, k12.

Round 13: Sl1, k2, psso, k8, k2tog, yo, k3, yo, ssk, k8, sl1, k2, psso.

Round 15: K10, k2tog, yo, k2, yo, ssk, k1, yo, ssk, k10.

Round 17: Sl1, k2, psso, k9, yo, ssk, k1, k2tog, yo, k9, sl1, k2, psso.

Round 19: K13, yo, cdd, yo, k13.

Round 20: Knit.

Key

☐	knit
O	yo
╱	k2tog
╲	ssk
∧	cdd
├──┤	sl1, k2, psso

Lace pattern (sizes M/L and XL)

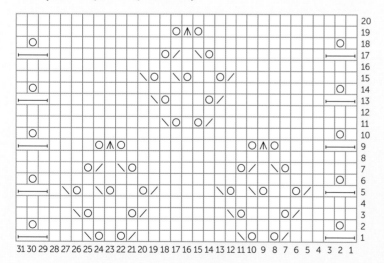

Round 1 (RS): Sl1, k2, psso, k3, k2tog, yo, k1, yo, ssk, k9, k2tog, yo, k1, yo, ssk, k3, sl1, k2, psso.

Rounds 2, 6, 10, 14 and 18: K1, yo, k27, yo, k1.

Round 3: K5, k2tog, yo, k3, yo, ssk, k7, k2tog, yo, k3, yo, ssk, k5.

Rounds 4, 8, 12 and 16: Knit.

Round 5: Sl1, k2, psso, k1, k2tog, yo, k2, yo, ssk, k1, yo, ssk, k5, k2tog, yo, k2, yo, ssk, k1, yo, ssk, k1, sl1, k2, psso.

Round 7: K6, yo, ssk, k1, k2tog, yo, k9, yo, ssk, k1, k2tog, yo, k6.

Round 9: Sl1, k2, psso, k4, yo, cdd, yo, k11, yo, cdd, yo, k4, sl1, k2, psso.

Round 11: K13, k2tog, yo, k1, yo, ssk, k13.

Round 13: Sl1, k2, psso, k9, k2tog, yo, k3, yo, ssk, k9, sl1, k2, psso.

Round 15: K11, k2tog, yo, k2, yo, ssk, k1, yo, ssk, k11.

Round 17: Sl1, k2, psso, k10, yo, ssk, k1, k2tog, yo, k10, sl1, k2, psso.

Round 19: K14, yo, cdd, yo, k14.

Round 20: Knit.

Instructions

Cuff

Using German twisted cast on (see Sock techniques: Casting on) or your preferred stretchy method, loosely cast on 56 [64] [72] sts onto 1 DPN.

Rib round: (K1tbl, p1) to the end. Do not turn your work (keep the RS of knitting facing you).

Next, starting from the opposite end of the DPN to the working yarn, carefully slip the stitches purlwise onto a short circular needle (or spread your stitches evenly over 4 DPNs), keeping RS of work facing at all times. Join to start knitting in the round (see Knitting in the round: Joining the round). Place a stitch marker in the first or last stitch of the round, moving it up as you work.

Continue in rib pattern (repeating Rib round) until you have completed 12 rounds in total or desired length.

Leg

Set-up round: K29 [31] [35], place marker, k27 [33] [37].

Round 1: K0 [0] [2], work Round 1 of Lace pattern from chart or written instructions for your size, k0 [0] [2], slip marker, knit to end of round.

Round 2: K0 [0] [2], work Round 2 of Lace pattern, k0 [0] [2], slip marker, knit to end of round.

Continue in pattern as set with Lace pattern on front of leg and stocking (stockinette) on back of leg.

Work until you have completed Rounds 1-20 three times in total.

Heel flap

The heel flap is worked on the last 27 [33] [37] sts of the round. Turn work to begin heel flap from WS, and leave 29 [31] [35] sts of front of leg on a stitch holder or spare needle.

Change to DPNs if you are using a short circular needle.

Row 1 (WS): P27 [33] [37], turn.

Row 2: (Sl1, k1) to last st, sl1, turn.

Repeat Rows 1-2 a total of 14 [16] [18] times, then work Row 1 once more.

Heel turn

Row 1 (RS): Sl1, k15 [19] [21], ssk, k1, turn.

Row 2: Sl1, p6 [8] [8], p2tog, p1, turn.

Row 3: Sl1, knit to 1 st before gap, ssk, k1, turn.

Row 4: Sl1, purl to 1 st before gap, p2tog, p1, turn.

Repeat Rows 3-4 until all heel sts have been worked. (17 [21] [23] heel sts)

Gusset

With RS facing, sl1, k16 [20] [22] heel sts, pick up and knit 14 [16] [18] sts along the edge of the heel flap, place stitch marker for new end of round, work next round of Lace pattern across instep sts, place marker, pick up and knit 14 [16] [18] sts up the other edge of the heel flap, knit to end of round. (74 [84] [94] sts)

Gusset shaping

Decrease round: Work next round of Lace pattern across instep sts, slip marker, k1, ssk, knit to last 3 sts, k2tog, k1. (2 gusset sts decreased)

Next round: Work next round of Lace pattern across instep sts, slip marker, knit to end of round.

Repeat the last 2 rounds until 56 [64] [72] sts remain.

Foot

Continue straight as set, working lace on instep and stocking (stockinette) stitch on sole sts, until the sock measures approximately 3.5 [4] [4]cm (1⅜ [1½] [1½] in) less than the desired foot length (see All about socks: Choosing the correct size), ending after a Round 10 or Round 20 of pattern.

If you need a few more rows after a Round 10 or Round 20 before shaping the toe, continue to work the mock cable detail at each side of the instep but work the centre sts in stocking (stockinette) stitch.

Toe

Size XS/S: Set-up round: Knit to 1 st before marker, place marker, k1, remove marker, knit to end of round.

Sizes M/L and XL: Set-up round: Knit to marker, remove marker, k1, place marker, knit to end of round.

ALL SIZES:

You should have 28 [32] [36] sts on each side of the markers.

If you are using a short circular needle, you will need to change to DPNs when there are too few sts on the circular needle.

Round 1: *K1, ssk, knit to 3 sts before marker, k2tog, k1; repeat from * once more. (4 sts decreased)

Rounds 2-3: Knit to end of round, slipping markers.

Rounds 4-6: Repeat Rounds 1-3 once more. (48 [56] [64] sts)

Round 7: Repeat Round 1.

Round 8: Knit to end of round, slipping markers.

Rounds 9-12: Repeat Rounds 7-8 twice more. (36 [44] [52] sts)

Round 13: Repeat Round 1.

Repeat Round 13 for a further 4 [5] [7] times. (16 [20] [20] sts)

To finish

Divide sts over 2 DPNs and use Kitchener stitch to graft toes together. Weave in all ends and trim. Block your socks and leave to dry completely (see Sock techniques: Finishing your project).

Bracken Cables

BY OLIVIA VILLAREAL

Jump right in with easy cables. The cable and twisted rib pattern for these socks starts at the top of the cuff, with 2-stitch cables on a reverse stocking (stockinette) stitch background. The twisted stitches give the cables great texture.

You will need

Yarn

Regia 4 Ply Merino Yak; 58% Merino wool, 28% polyamide, 14% yak; 400m (437 yards) per 110g (3.9oz) ball

1 ball in Gold Meliert

This yarn is a 4ply (fingering) weight yarn, so any similar weight yarn would work well (see Checking your tension/ gauge: Substituting yarn).

Needles

2.5mm (US2 or US1) needles for your preferred method of knitting in the round

If using a short circular needle, you will also need a set of DPNs in the same size for the cast on, heels and toes

Extras

Cable needle; tape measure or ruler; stitch markers; stitch holder (optional); tapestry/ yarn needle (for weaving in ends); sock blockers (optional), towel and wool wash for blocking (see Tools and materials: Extras)

Tension/Gauge

32 sts and 42 rows to 10 x 10cm (4 x 4in) measured in stocking (stockinette) stitch using 2.5mm (US2 or US1) needles

If you need to use a different needle size to achieve this tension/gauge, make sure to use that needle size throughout (see Checking your tension/gauge).

Sizes

XS/S [M/L] [XL]

Knitted sock, actual knitted circumference:

18 [20.5] [23]cm (7 [8] [9]in)

Will stretch to fit approximate foot circumference:

19 [21.5] [24] cm (7½ [8½] [9½]in)

Construction

Cuff-down: these socks are cast on at the cuff and the **leg** pattern begins immediately.

Heel flap & gusset: the heel is knitted on half of the stitches and worked in rows (to create a rectangular **heel flap**) in slipstitch (see Sock elements: Heels), then simple short rows are used to shape the **heel turn**. Stitches are picked up along each side of the heel flap and the **gusset** is worked in the round, decreasing at each side of the foot for the gusset shaping.

Foot: the **foot** is then worked in rounds with the pattern continued on the instep.

Toe: the classic wedge **toe** (see Sock elements: Toes) is shaped with simple decreases and the toe seam is closed with a Kitchener stitch **graft**.

Project notes

Due to the pattern repeat, note that the sizes differ from the recipes so make sure to check the sizing to determine which size will best fit your foot (see All about socks: Choosing the correct size).

Special abbreviations

C2Ftbl, place next stitch on cable needle, hold at front, k1tbl from left-hand needle, k1tbl from cable needle

T2B, place next stitch on cable needle, hold at back, k1tbl from left-hand needle, p1 from cable needle

T2F, place next stitch on cable needle, hold at front, p1 from left-hand needle, k1tbl from cable needle

Stitch patterns

Cable and twisted rib - size XS/S (58 sts)

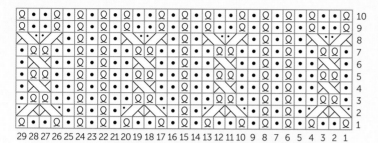

Round 1: *K1tbl, p2, (k1tbl, p1) 3 times, k1tbl, p2, (k1tbl, p1) twice, k1tbl, p2, (k1tbl, p1) 3 times, k1tbl, p2, k1tbl; repeat from * once more.

Round 2: *T2F, T2B, p1, k1tbl, (p1, k1tbl, p1, T2F, T2B) twice, (p1, k1tbl) twice, p1, T2F, T2B; repeat from * once more.

Round 3: *P1, k2tbl, p2, k1tbl, p1, (k1tbl, p2, k2tbl, p2) twice, k1tbl, p1, k1tbl, p2, k2tbl, p1; repeat from * once more.

Round 4: *P1, C2Ftbl, p2, k1tbl, p1, (k1tbl, p2, C2Ftbl, p2) twice, k1tbl, p1, k1tbl, p2, C2Ftbl, p1; repeat from * once more.

Round 5-6: Repeat Rounds 3-4.

Rounds 7: Repeat Round 3.

Round 8: *T2B, T2F, p1, k1tbl, (p1, k1tbl, p1, T2B, T2F) twice, (p1, k1tbl) twice, p1, T2B, T2F; repeat from * once more.

Rounds 9-10: *K1tbl, p2, (k1tbl, p1) 3 times, k1tbl, p2, (k1tbl, p1) twice, k1tbl, p2, (k1tbl, p1) 3 times, k1tbl, p2, k1tbl; repeat from * once more.

Cable and twisted rib - size M/L (66 sts)

Round 1: *(P1, k1tbl, p2, k1tbl, p1, k1tbl, p1, k1tbl) 3 times, p1, k1tbl, p2, k1tbl, p1; repeat from * once more.

Round 2: *(P1, T2F, T2B, p1, k1tbl, p1, k1tbl) 3 times, p1, T2F, T2B, p1; repeat from * once more.

Round 3: *(P2, k1tbl twice, p2, k1tbl, p1, k1tbl) 3 times, p2, k1tbl twice, p2; repeat from * once more.

Round 4: *(P2, C2Ftbl, p2, k1tbl, p1, k1tbl) 3 times, p2, C2Ftbl, p2; repeat from * once more.

Round 5-6: Repeat Rounds 3-4.

Rounds 7: Repeat Round 3.

Round 8: *(P1, T2B, T2F, p1, k1tbl, p1, k1tbl) 3 times, p1, T2B, T2F, p1; repeat from * once more.

Rounds 9-10: *(P1, k1tbl, p2, k1tbl, p1, k1tbl, p1, k1tbl) 3 times, p1, k1tbl, p2, k1tbl, p1; repeat from * once more.

Cable and twisted rib - size XL (74 sts)

Round 1: *(P1, k1tbl, p1, k1tbl, p2, k1tbl, p1, k1tbl) 4 times, p1; repeat from * once more.

Round 2: *(P1, k1tbl, p1, T2F, T2B, p1, k1tbl) 4 times, p1; repeat from * once more.

Round 3: *(P1, k1tbl, p2, k2tbl, p2, k1tbl) 4 times, p1; repeat from * once more.

Round 4: *(P1, k1tbl, p2, C2Ftbl, p2, k1tbl) 4 times, p1; repeat from * once more.

Round 5-6: Repeat Rounds 3-4.

Rounds 7: Repeat Round 3.

Round 8: *(P1, k1tbl, p1, T2B, T2F, p1, k1tbl) 4 times, p1; repeat from * once more.

Rounds 9-10: *(P1, k1tbl, p1, k1tbl, p2, k1tbl, p1, k1tbl) 4 times, p1; repeat from * once more.

Key

Q	knit
•	purl
⟋⟍	C2Ftbl
⟋	T2B
⟍	T2F

Instructions

Cuff

Using German twisted cast on (see Sock techniques: Casting on) or your preferred stretchy method, loosely cast on 58 [68] [74] sts onto 1 DPN.

Rib round: (K1tbl, p1) to the end. Do not turn your work (keep the RS of knitting facing you).

Next, starting from the opposite end of the DPN to the working yarn, carefully slip the stitches purlwise onto a short circular needle (or spread your stitches evenly over 4 DPNs), keeping RS of work facing at all times. Join to start knitting in the round (see Knitting in the round: Joining the round). Place a stitch marker in the first or last stitch of the round, moving it up as you work.

There are no additional rib rounds as the leg begins immediately.

Leg

Repeat Round 1-10 of Cable and twisted rib pattern for your size from chart or written instructions 6 times in total or until desired leg length. If you are working from the charts, work each chart row twice each round.

Heel flap

Change to DPNs if you are using a short circular needle.

The heel flap is worked on the first half of the stitches, with an extra stitch increased to have an even number of sts for the heel flap.

Set-up row (RS): Sl1, M1L, (sl1, k1) until you have 30 [34] [38] sts on your needle, turn.

You can place the remaining sts on a stitch holder or spare needle while you work if you prefer.

Row 1: Sl1, purl to end, turn.

Row 2: (Sl1, k1) to end, turn.

Repeat Rows 1-2 a total of 15 [17] [19] times, then repeat Row 2 once more.

Heel turn

Row 1 (RS): K17 [19] [21], ssk, k1, turn.

Row 2: Sl1, p5, p2tog, p1, turn.

Row 3: Sl1, knit to 1 st before gap, ssk, k1, turn.

Row 4: Sl1, purl to 1 st before gap, p2tog, p1, turn.

Repeat Rows 3-4 until all heel sts have been worked. (18 [20] [22] heel sts)

Gusset

With RS facing, k9 [10] [11] heel sts, place new marker for end of round, k9 [10] [11] heel sts, pick up and knit 15 [17] [19] sts along the edge of the heel flap, place stitch marker, work instep sts in Cable and twisted rib pattern as set, place marker, pick up and knit 15 [17] [19] sts up the other edge of the heel flap, knit to end of round. (77 [87] [97] sts)

Gusset shaping

Round 1: Knit to 3 sts before the marker, k2tog, k1, slip marker, work instep sts in Cable and twisted rib pattern as set, slip marker, k1, ssk, knit to end of round. (2 sts decreased)

Round 2: Knit to marker, slip marker, work instep sts in Cable and twisted rib pattern as set, slip marker, knit to end of round.

Repeat the last 2 rounds until 59 [67] [75] sts remain.

Foot

Next round: K2tog, knit to marker, slip marker, work instep sts in Cable and twisted rib pattern as set, slip marker, knit to end of round. (58 [66] [74] sts)

Continue straight, working in Cable and twisted rib pattern on instep between markers and stocking (stockinette) stitch on sole sts, until the sock measures 4.5 [5] [5.5] cm (1¾ [2] [2¼]in) less than the desired foot length (see All about socks: Choosing the correct size), ending after a Round 1, 9 or 10 of pattern.

Toe

If you are using a short circular needle, you will need to change to DPNs when there are too few sts on the circular needle.

Next round (partial): Remove start of round marker, knit to next marker. This is the new start of round marker.

Round 1: *K1, ssk, knit to 3 sts before next marker, k2tog, k1; repeat from * once more. (4 sts decreased)

Round 2: Knit to end of round, slipping markers.

Repeat Rounds 1-2 until 22 [22] [26] sts remain.

To finish

Divide sts over 2 DPNs and use Kitchener stitch to graft toes together. Weave in all ends and trim. Block your socks and leave to dry completely (see Sock techniques: Finishing your project).

Summer Meadows

BY CARMEN JORISSEN

These toe-up socks were inspired by the traditional Fair Isle XO motifs, with a striping effect created by alternating pairs of contrasting colours. You never need to work with more than 2 colours in a row. With contrast heel, toe and cuff, these socks are a beautiful way to play with a palette of colour.

You will need

Yarn
4 colours of yarn are used:

Scheepjes Metropolis; 75% Merino wool, 25% nylon; 200m (216 yards) per 50g (1.75oz) skein

1 skein each in Milan 057 (Yarn A), Dubai 047 (Yarn B), Marrakech 051 (Yarn C) and Sydney 048 (Yarn D)

This yarn is a 4ply (fingering) weight yarn, so any similar weight yarn would work well (see Checking your tension/ gauge: Substituting yarn).

Each colour pair should contrast well together (Yarn A as pattern colour to contrast with Yarn B as background colour, Yarn C as pattern colour to contrast with Yarn D as background colour). Make a small swatch before you begin to check your colour choices.

Needles
2.25mm (US1) and 2.5mm (US2 or US1) needles for your preferred method of knitting in the round

Check both your colourwork tension and stocking (stockinette) tension. Some knitters may find no difference in tension for colourwork and should then use the same needles throughout.

Extras
Tape measure or ruler; stitch markers (1 distinct round marker and 2 distinct markers for gusset); stitch holder (optional); tapestry/ yarn needle; sock blockers (optional), towel and wool wash for blocking (see Tools and materials: Extras)

Tension/Gauge
34 sts and 36 rows to 10 x 10cm (4 x 4in) measured in colourwork pattern using 2.5mm (US2 or US1) needles

34 sts and 36 rows to 10 x 10cm (4 x 4in) measured in stocking (stockinette) stitch using 2.25mm (US1) needles

If you need to use different needle sizes to achieve either tension/gauge, make sure to use that needle size whenever needed (see Checking your tension/gauge).

Sizes
XS [S/M] [L] [XL]

Knitted sock, actual knitted circumference:
16.5 [19] [21] [23.5]cm (6½ [7½] [8¼] [9¼]in)

Will stretch to fit approximate foot circumference:
17.5 [20] [22] [24.5]cm (6¾ [8] [8¾] [9¾]in)

Construction

Toe-up: these socks are cast on at the toe with a closed cast-on. The **toe** is a wedge toe shaped with simple increases and the **foot** is worked in stranded colourwork worked from the chart.

Gusset & heel flap: a striped **gusset** is worked in the round, shaped with increases in the same colours as the main pattern. The heel is knitted on less than half of the stitches using double stitch short rows (see Sock techniques: Short rows) for the heel turn. The **heel flap** is worked in rows that incorporate and decrease away the gusset sts as the rectangular area is shaped and attached at the same time (see Sock elements: Heels).

Leg: the colourwork pattern is continued up the **leg**, which can be adjusted for length.

Cuff: beginning with a garter stitch ridge, the **cuff** is mainly worked in half-twisted 1 x 1 rib, then cast (bind) off using a stretchy cast (bind) off.

Project notes

In the gusset instructions, pattern colour refers to Yarn A and Yarn C and background colour refers to Yarn B and Yarn D. These terms are used as the length of your foot will determine which chart round begins the gusset. To knit in pattern within the striped gusset, if the next stitch on left-hand needle is a pattern colour (Yarn A or Yarn C), work it in the current pattern colour; if the next stitich on left-hand needle is a background colour (Yarn B or Yarn D), work it in the current background colour.

Special abbreviations

BC, background colour (Yarn B or Yarn D)

PC, pattern colour (Yarn A or Yarn C)

Instructions

Toe

With Yarn A and 2.25mm (US1) needles, cast on 20 [20] [24] [24] sts using a closed cast on method such as Judy's magic cast on (see Sock techniques: Casting on). Place stitch marker after stitch 10 [10] [12] [12] and in the first or last st of the round.

Round 1: Knit to end of round.

Round 2: Kfb, knit to last st before marker, kfb, sm, kfb, knit to last st of round, kfb. (4 sts increased)

Repeat Rounds 1-2 until there are 56 [64] [72] [80] sts.

Next round: Knit to end of round.

Key

- ■ Yarn A
- ■ Yarn B
- ■ Yarn C
- □ Yarn D
- ☐ repeat

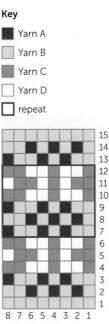

Foot

Change to larger needles and join in Yarn B, Yarn C and Yarn D as needed.

Carry your unused yarn along the inside of the sock and work in stranded colourwork from the chart (see Sock techniques: Reading charts, and Working with more than one yarn/colour) as follows:

Repeating sts 7 [8] [9] [10] times to end of round, work Rounds 1-12 of chart.

Do not cut yarn between rounds. Instead, carry the unneeded colours up along the start of the round loosely, switching the pairs of colours every 3 rows as needed.

Repeating only Rounds 7-12 of chart, work until the sock measures 6 [6] [6.5] [6.5]cm (2¼ [2¼] [2½] [2½]in) less than the desired foot length (see All about socks: Choosing the correct sock size).

Gusset shaping

Continue in colourwork pattern, working gusset sts in pattern or background colour (see project notes) as instructed between markers.

Round 1. Knit in patt to marker, sm, k1 in patt, pm for gusset, M1L with BC (Yarn B or Yarn D depending on what pattern round you are on), pm, knit in patt to last st, pm for gusset, M1R with BC, pm, k1 in patt. (2 sts increased)

Round 2: Knit in patt to marker, sm, k1 in patt, sm, k1 gusset st with BC, sm, knit in patt to marker, sm, k1 gusset st with BC, sm, k1 in patt.

Round 3: Knit in patt to marker, sm, k1 in patt, sm, M1L with BC, k1 gusset st with BC, sm, knit in patt to marker, sm, k1 gusset st with BC, M1R with BC, sm, k1 in patt.

Round 4: Knit in colourwork and gusset patts as set to end of round, slipping markers.

Round 5: Knit in patt to marker, sm, k1 in patt, sm, k1 gusset st with BC, M1L in PC, knit gusset sts in patt to marker, sm, knit in patt to marker, sm, knit gusset sts in patt to last st before marker, M1R in PC, k1 gusset st in BC, sm, k1 in patt.

Round 6: Repeat Round 4.

Round 7: Knit in patt to marker, sm, k1 in patt, sm, k1 gusset st with BC, M1L in BC, knit gusset sts in patt to marker, sm, knit in patt to marker, sm, knit gusset sts in patt to last st before marker, M1R in BC, k1 gusset st in BC, sm, k1 in patt.

Repeat Rounds 4-7 until you have 11 [11] [13] [13] sts for each gusset. (78 [86] [98] [106] sts)

If necessary, work a few rounds straight in patts as set until sock measures desired foot length (see All about socks: Choosing the correct size).

Heel turn

Set-up row (RS): Knit in patt to marker, sm, k1 in patt, sm, knit gusset sts in patt to marker, sm.

Cut current BC yarn.

The heel turn is worked with PC on the next 26 [30] [34] [38] sts before the next gusset marker, using double stitch short rows (see Sock techniques: Short rows). If you prefer to use a different colour for the heel, cut the yarn and join in your preferred colour.

Change to 2.25mm (US1) needles.

You can leave remaining sts on the 2.5mm (US2 or US1) needles after Row 1 and work heel sts back and forth on the 2.25mm (US1) needles.

Row 1 (RS): With PC or preferred colour, k26 [30] [34] [38], turn.

Row 2: MDS, p25 [29] [33] [37], turn.

Row 3: MDS, knit to previous DS, turn.

Row 4: MDS, purl to previous DS, turn.

Repeat Rows 3-4 until there are 15 [15] [13] [13] sts left between the double stitches, ending after a WS row.

Next row (RS): MDS, k14 [14] [12] [12], knit DS as a single st, turn.

Next row: MDS, purl to previous DS, purl DS as a single st, turn.

Next row: MDS, knit to previous DS, knit DS as a single st, turn.

Repeat these 2 rows until all DS have been worked, ending after a WS row.

Heel flap

At the end of each heel flap row, you will be decreasing gusset sts. Make sure to remove the gusset marker before working the decreases in the first 2 rows.

Row 1 (RS): Sl1, knit until 1 st before the gap between the heel sts and the gusset sts, ssk together the last heel st and the first gusset st, turn. (1 st decreased)

Change to 2.5mm (US2 or US1) needles.

You can simply begin using the needle the gusset sts are being held on and drop the 2.25mm (US1) needle on the next pass.

Row 2: Sl1, (p1, sl1) until 1 st before the gap between the heel sts and gusset sts, p2tog (using last heel st and first gusset st), turn. (1 st decreased)

Row 3: Sl1, (k1, sl1) until 1 st before the gap between the heel sts and gusset sts, ssk (using last heel st and first gusset st), turn. (1 st decreased)

Repeat Rows 2-3 until all of the gusset sts have been decreased. On final RS row, do not turn, work next st in patt to start of round marker. You will have 28 [32] [36] [40] sts between the remaining markers. (56 [64] [72] [80] sts)

Leg

Re-join BC cut at start of heel turn as needed.

Continue working in colourwork patt as set, repeating Rows 7-12 from where you left off for the heel until leg measures 4cm (1½in) less than desired length.

Work Rows 13-15 of chart to complete colourwork before the cuff.

Cuff

Change to smaller needles and cut all yarns except Yarn A.

Round 1: Knit to end of round.

Round 2: Purl to end of round.

Round 3: Knit to end of round.

Rounds 4-10: (K1tbl, p1) to end of round.

Cast off all sts using a stretchy cast off, such as Jeny's surprisingly stretchy cast (bind) off (see Sock techniques: Casting (binding) off).

To finish

Weave in all ends and trim. Block your socks and leave to dry completely (see Sock techniques: Finishing your project).

Autumn Berries

BY KAITLIN BARTHOLD

Worked in a mesh-like lace, these socks are worked cuff down. Step up your sock skills while showing off a special yarn to great effect.

You will need

Yarn
Kenyarn Cirrus Fingering; 75% Merino superwash wool 25% nylon; 424m (463 yards) per 100g (3.5oz) skein

1 skein in Mauve

This yarn is a 4ply (fingering) weight yarn, so any similar weight yarn would work well (see Checking your tension/gauge: Substituting yarn).

Needles
2.25mm (US1) needles for your preferred method of knitting in the round

If using a short circular needle, you will also need a set of DPNs in the same size for the cast on, heels and toes

Extras
Tape measure or ruler; stitch markers; stitch holder (optional); tapestry/yarn needle (for weaving in ends); pair of sock blockers (optional), towel and wool wash for blocking (see Tools and materials: Extras)

Tension/Gauge
32 sts and 44 rows to 10 x 10cm (4 x 4in) measured in stocking (stockinette) stitch using 2.25mm (US1) needles

If you need to use a different needle size to achieve this tension/gauge, make sure to use that needle size throughout (see Checking your tension/gauge).

Sizes
XS/S [M/L] [XL] [2XL]

Knitted sock, actual knitted circumference:
17.5 [20] [22.5] [25]cm (7 [7¾] [8¾] [9¾]in)

Will stretch to fit approximate foot circumference:
18.5 [21] [23.5] [26]cm (7¼ [8¼] [9¼] [10¼]in)

Construction

Cuff-down: these socks are cast on at the cuff and worked in the round to the heel. The **cuff** is a 1 x 1 rib and the **leg** is a lace pattern worked from the chart or written instructions.

Heel flap & gusset: the heel is knitted on odd number of approximately half of the stitches, and worked in rows (to create a rectangular **heel flap**) in slipstitch (see Sock elements: Heels), then simple short rows are used to shape the **heel turn**. Stitches are picked up along each side of the heel flap and the **gusset** is worked in the round, decreasing at each side of the foot for the gusset shaping.

Foot: the **foot** is then worked in rounds with the lace pattern continued on just the instep sts.

Toe: the classic wedge **toe** (see Sock elements: Toes) is shaped with simple decreases and the toe seam is closed with a Kitchener stitch **graft**.

Project notes

Because of the pattern repeat and tension/gauge, note that there are fewer sizes than the recipes – make sure to check the sizing to determine which size will best fit your foot. The heel flap is worked over an odd number of stitches so pay attention when instructed to turn for the heel. The heel of the cuff-down recipe is similar to this, and the toe is the same, so you can use the step-by-step guides there for a refresher if needed (see Sock recipes: Cuff-down socks). Note that the stitch count varies over different rounds for the lace pattern.

Stitch patterns

Leg lace pattern

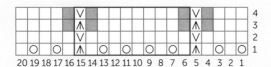

20	19	18	17	16	15	14	13	12	11	10	9	8	7	6	5	4	3	2	1	

(Chart rows numbered 4, 3, 2, 1)

Round 1: (Yo, k1) twice, cdd, *(k1, yo) 4 times, k1, cdd; repeat from * to last 3 sts, (k1, yo) twice, k1. (70 [80] [90] [100] sts)

Round 2: K4, sl1, (k9, sl1) to last 5 sts, k5.

Round 3: K3, cdd, (k7, cdd) to last 4 sts, k4. (56 [64] [72] [80] sts)

Round 4: K3, sl1, (k7, sl1) to last 4 sts, k4.

Key

- ☐ knit
- V sl1
- ⋀ cdd
- ⵔ yo
- ⟍ ssk
- ⟋ k2tog
- ☐ k1 [3] [1] [3]
- ▦ no stitch
- ☐ repeat

Instep lace pattern

23	22	21	20	19	18	17	16	15	14	13	12	11	10	9	8	7	6	5	4	3	2	1	

(Chart rows numbered 4, 3, 2, 1)

Round 1: K1 [3] [1] [3], ssk, *k1, (yo, k1) 4 times, cdd; repeat from * 1 [1] [2] [2] more times, k1, (yo, k1) 4 times, k2tog, k1 [3] [1] [3].

Round 2: K1 [3] [1] [3], sl1, (k9, sl1) 3 [3] [4] [4] times, k1 [3] [1] [3].

Round 3: K1 [3] [1] [3], ssk, (k7, cdd) 2 [2] [3] [3] times, k7, k2tog, k1 [3] [1] [3].

Round 4: K1 [3] [1] [3], (k7, sl1) 3 [3] [4] [4] times, k1 [3] [1] [3].

Instructions

Cuff

Loosely cast on 56 [64] [72] [80] sts onto 1 DPN.

Rib round: (K1, p1) to the end. Do not turn your work (keep the RS of knitting facing you).

Next, starting from the opposite end of the DPN to the working yarn, carefully slip the stitches purlwise onto a short circular needle (or spread your stitches evenly over 4 DPNs), keeping RS of work facing at all times. Join to start knitting in the round (see Knitting in the round: Joining the round). Place a stitch marker in the first or last stitch of the round, moving it up as you work.

Continue in rib pattern (repeating Rib round) until you have completed 10 rounds in total or desired length.

Leg

Next round: Knit.

Repeat Rounds 1-4 of Leg lace pattern from chart or written instructions until sock measures 10cm (4in) or preferred length, ending after a Round 3 of lace pattern.

See Sock techniques: Decreasing, for an illustrated guide to working cdd, a central double decrease.

Heel flap

Set-up round: Work as for Round 4 of Leg lace pattern, stopping 2 [0] [2] [0] sts before end of round. For sizes XS/S and XL, this is the new end of round.

Change to DPNs if you are using a short circular needle.

Row 1 (RS): K1, (sl1, k1) until you have 27 [31] [35] [39] sts on your needle, turn.

The remaining 29 [33] [37] [41] sts are for the instep. You can place these on a stitch holder or spare needle while you work if you prefer.

Row 2: Sl1, purl to last st, sl1, turn.

Row 3: K1, (sl1, k1) to end, turn.

Repeat Rows 2-3 a total of 12 [14] [16] [18] times, then repeat Row 2 once more.

Heel turn

Row 1 (RS): K15 [17] [19] [21], ssk, k1, turn.

Row 2: Sl1, p4, p2tog, p1, turn.

Row 3: Sl1, knit to 1 st before gap, ssk, k1, turn.

Row 4: Sl1, purl to 1 st before gap, p2tog, p1, turn.

Repeat Rows 3-4 until all heel sts have been worked. Depending on the number of sts you started with, you may need to end the final 2 rows with ssk and p2tog. (15 [17] [19] [21] heel sts)

Gusset

With RS facing, sl1, k14 [16] [18] [20] heel sts, place marker for new end of round, pick up and knit 16 [18] [20] [22] sts along the edge of the heel flap, knit first instep st, place stitch marker, work Round 1 of Instep lace pattern from chart or written instructions to last instep st, place marker, knit last instep st, pick up and knit 16 [18] [20] [22] sts up the other edge of the heel flap, knit to end of round. (80 [90] [102] [112] sts)

Next round: Working picked-up sts along heel flap tbl, knit to 2 sts before marker, k2tog, slip marker, work next round of Instep lace pattern, slip marker, ssk, working picked-up sts along heel flap tbl, knit to end of round. (2 gusset sts decreased)

Gusset shaping

Next round: Knit to marker, slip marker, work next round of Instep lace pattern, slip marker, knit to end of round.

Decrease round: Knit to 2 sts before marker, k2tog, slip marker, work next round of Instep lace pattern, slip marker, ssk, knit to end of round. (2 gusset sts decreased)

Repeat the last 2 rounds until 56 [64] [72] [80] sts remain.

Foot

Set-up round (partial): Remove start of round marker, knit to marker, this is the new start of round marker.

Next round: Work Instep lace pattern to next marker, slip marker, knit to end of round.

Continue straight as set, working lace on instep and stocking (stockinette) stitch on sole sts, until the sock measures approximately 4cm (1½in) less than the desired foot length (see All about socks: Choosing the correct size).

Toe

If you are using a short circular needle, you will need to change to DPNs when there are too few sts on the circular needle.

Round 1: *K1, ssk, knit to 3 sts before marker, k2tog, k1; repeat from * once more. (4 sts decreased)

Round 2: Knit to end of round, slipping markers.

Repeat Rounds 1-2 for a further 7 times. (24 [32] [40] [48] sts)

Repeat Round 1 twice more. (16 [24] [32] [40] sts)

To finish

Divide sts over 2 DPNs and use Kitchener stitch to graft toes together. Weave in all ends and trim. Block your socks and leave to dry completely (see Sock techniques: Finishing your project).

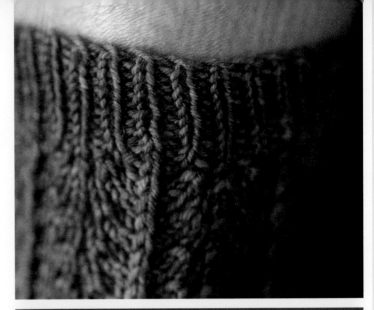

Red Sky At Night

BY ABBY BROWN

These cuff-down socks feature a bold art deco stranded colourwork pattern on the leg and foot. Make sure to select 2 colours with a good contrast for a visual punch.

You will need

Yarn
2 colours of yarn are needed:

Cascade Yarns Heritage; 75% Merino superwash wool, 25% nylon; 400m (437 yards) per 100g (3.5oz) skein

1 skein each in Chanterelle (Yarn A) and Navy (Yarn B)

This yarn is a 4ply (fingering) weight yarn, so any similar weight yarn would work well (see Checking your tension/gauge: Substituting yarn).

Needles
2.25mm (US1) and 2.75mm (US2) needles for your preferred method of knitting in the round

If using a short circular needle, you will also need a set of DPNs in the same size for the cast on, heels and toes

You can use the larger needles for the colourwork sections, but it's a good idea to check your colourwork tension as well as your stocking (stockinette) tension. Some knitters may find they don't have any difference in tension for colourwork – if this is true for you, use the same needles throughout.

Extras
Tape measure or ruler; stitch markers; stitch holder (optional); tapestry/yarn needle; sock blockers (optional), towel and wool wash for blocking (see Tools and materials: Extras)

Tension/Gauge
36 sts and 36 rows to 10 x 10cm (4 x 4in) measured in colourwork pattern using 2.75mm (US2) needles

36 sts and 36 rows to 10 x 10cm (4 x 4in) measured in stocking (stockinette) stitch using 2.25mm (US1) needles

If you need to use a different needle size to achieve either tension/gauge, make sure to use that needle size whenever needed (see Checking your tension/gauge).

Sizes
XS/S [M/L] [XL] [2XL]

Knitted sock, actual knitted circumference:
17.5 [20] [22.5] [24.5]cm
(7 [7¾] [8¾] [9½]in)

Will stretch to fit approximate foot circumference:
18.5 [21] [23.5] [25.5]cm
(7½ [8¼] [9¼] [10]in)

Construction

Cuff-down: these socks are cast on at the cuff and worked in the round to the heel. The **cuff** is a 2 x 2 rib and the **leg** is a stranded colourwork pattern worked from the chart.

Heel flap & gusset: the heel is knitted on half of the stitches and worked in rows (to create a rectangular **heel flap**) in slipstitch (see Sock elements: Heels), then simple short rows are used to shape the **heel turn**. Stitches are picked up along each side of the heel flap and the **gusset** is worked in the round, decreasing at each side of the foot for the gusset shaping.

Foot: the **foot** is then worked in rounds with an additional band of stranded colourwork before the toe.

Toe: the classic wedge **toe** (see Sock elements: Toes) is shaped with simple decreases and the toe seam is closed with a Kitchener stitch **graft**.

Project notes

Because of the pattern repeat and tension/gauge, note that the sizes differ slightly from the recipes – make sure to check the sizing to determine which size will best fit your foot. The cuff-down recipe uses the same heel and toe as these socks, so you can use the step-by-step guides there for a refresher if needed (see Sock recipes: Cuff-down socks).

Instructions

Cuff

With Yarn B and smaller needles, loosely cast on 64 [72] [80] [88] sts onto 1 DPN.

Rib round: (K2, p2) to the end. Do not turn your work (keep the RS of knitting facing you).

Next, starting from the opposite end of the DPN to the working yarn, carefully slip the stitches purlwise onto a short circular needle (or spread your stitches evenly over 4 DPNs), keeping RS of work facing at all times. Join to start knitting in the round (see Knitting in the round: Joining the round). Place a stitch marker in the first or last stitch of the round, moving it up as you work.

Continue in rib pattern (repeating Rib round) until cuff measures 3.5cm (1½in) or desired length.

Leg

Change to larger needles and join in Yarn A as needed.

Carry your unused yarn along the inside of the sock and work in stranded colourwork from the chart (see Sock techniques: Reading charts, and Working with more than one yarn/colour) as follows:

Repeating sts 8 [9] [10] [11] times to end of round, work Rounds 1–40 of Leg chart.

You may find it useful to place stitch markers after each repeat.

Once chart is complete, cut Yarn B and continue with Yarn A only. Change to smaller needles and remove any pattern markers, but do not remove start of round marker.

Work in stocking (stockinette) stitch (knit every round) until leg measures 16.5cm (6½in) or your desired length.

Leg chart

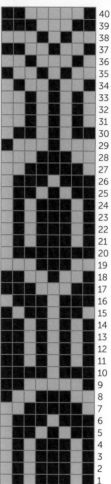

Foot chart

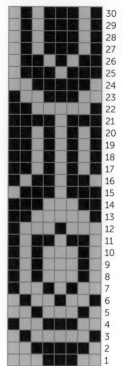

Key

■ Yarn A
■ Yarn B

Heel flap

Change to DPNs if you are using a short circular needle.

Row 1 (RS): (Sl1, k1) until you have 32 [36] [40] [44] sts on your needle, turn.

You can place the remaining sts on a stitch holder or spare needle while you work if you prefer.

Row 2: Sl1, purl to end, turn.

Row 3: (Sl1, k1) to end, turn.

Repeat Rows 2–3 a total of 16 [18] [20] [22] times.

Heel turn

Row 1 (WS): Sl1, p17 [19] [21] [23], p2tog, p1, turn.

Row 2: Sl1, k5, ssk, k1, turn.

Row 3: Sl1, purl to 1 st before gap, p2tog, p1, turn.

Row 4: Sl1, knit to 1 st before gap, ssk, k1, turn.

Repeat Rows 3–4 until all heel sts have been worked. Depending on the number of sts you started with, you may need to end the final 2 rows with p2tog and k2tog. Do not turn after the final RS row. (18 [20] [22] [24] heel sts)

Gusset

Continue with Yarn A, pick up and knit 16 [18] [20] [22] sts along the edge of the heel flap (see Sock techniques: Picking up stitches), pick up and knit 1 st from the gap between the end of the picked up sts and the instep sts by using M1R (see Sock techniques: Increasing), place stitch marker, knit 32 [36] [40] [44] instep sts, place marker at end of instep sts, pick up and knit 1 st from the gap before the heel flap by using M1L, then pick up and knit 16 [18] [20] [22] sts up the other edge of the heel flap.

Place another stitch marker to mark the new start of the round. (84 [94] [104] [114] sts)

Gusset shaping

Round 1: Knit to end of round.

Round 2: Knit to 3 sts before the marker, k2tog, k1, slip marker, knit instep sts, slip marker, k1, ssk, knit to end of round. (2 sts decreased)

Repeat the last 2 rounds until 64 [72] [80] [88] sts remain.

Foot

Continue working straight with Yarn A in stocking (stockinette) stitch until the sock measures approximately 14.5 [15] [15] [16]cm (5¾ [6] [6] [6¼]in) less than the desired foot length (see All about socks: Choosing the correct size).

Depending on your foot length, this may be just after you finish the gusset shaping.

Change to larger needles and join in Yarn B as needed.

Repeating sts 8 [9] [10] [11] times to end of round, work Rounds 1-30 of Foot chart.

Once chart is complete, cut Yarn A and continue with Yarn B only.

Toe

Change to smaller needles. If you are using a short circular needle, you will need to change to DPNs when there are too few sts on the circular needle.

Next round (partial): Remove start of round marker, knit to next marker. This is the new start of round marker.

Round 1: *K1, ssk, knit to 3 sts before next marker, k2tog, k1; repeat from * once more. (4 sts decreased)

Round 2: Knit to end of round, slipping markers.

Repeat Rounds 1-2 until 20 [24] [28] [32] sts remain.

To finish

Divide sts over 2 DPNs and use Kitchener stitch to graft toes together. Weave in all ends and trim. Block your socks and leave to dry completely (see Sock techniques: Finishing your project).

Beads of Dew

BY ANNIKEN ALLIS

Take your sock-knitting a step up by adding beads and lace to your project. Worked toe-up, you can work until these socks are the perfect leg length for you. A special variegated yarn works well for this design, but would look equally stunning in a solid colour with contrasting beads.

You will need

Yarn

Orchidean Luxury Yarns Titanium Sock; 75% Merino superwash wool, 25% nylon; 425m (465 yards) per 100g (3.5oz) skein

1 skein in Let there be more light

This yarn is a 4ply (fingering) weight yarn, so any similar weight yarn would work well (see Checking your tension/ gauge: Substituting yarn).

Needles

2.5mm (US2 or US1) needles for your preferred method of knitting in the round

If using a short circular needle, you will also need a set of DPNs in the same size for the toes

Extras

0.75mm (US14) crochet hook; 1 bag Debbie Abrahams size 6 beads (shown in colour 235); tape measure or ruler; stitch markers; tapestry/yarn needle; sock blockers (optional), towel and wool wash (see Tools and materials: Extras)

The exact size of the crochet hook isn't as important as making sure that the hook fits through the hole in the beads.

Tension/Gauge

30 sts and 44 rows to 10 x 10cm (4 x 4in) measured in lace pattern using 2.5mm (US2 or US1) needles

28 sts and 44 rows to 10 x 10cm (4 x 4in) measured in stocking (stockinette) stitch using 2.5mm (US2 or US1) needles

If you need to use a different needle size to achieve either tension/gauge, make sure to use that needle size whenever needed (see Checking your tension/gauge).

Sizes

XS/S [M] [L/XL] [2XL]

Knitted sock, actual knitted circumference:

16 [20] [22] [24]cm (6¼ [8] [8¾] [9½]in)

Will stretch to fit approximate foot circumference:

17 [21] [23] [25]cm (6¾ [8¼] [9] [9¾]in)

Construction

Toe-up: these socks are cast on at the toe with a closed cast-on. The **toe** is a wedge toe shaped with simple increases and the **foot** is worked with the sole in stocking (stockinette) stitch and the instep (top of foot) worked in bead and lace pattern.

Gusset & heel flap: a **gusset** is worked in the round, shaped with increases. The heel is knitted on half of the stitches using double stitch short rows (see Sock techniques: Short rows) for the **heel turn**. The **heel flap** is worked in rows that incorporate and decrease away the gusset sts as the rectangular area is shaped and attached at the same time (see Sock elements: Heels).

Leg: the bead and lace pattern is continued up the **leg** on all sts, with adjustable length.

Cuff: the **cuff** is worked in 1 x 1 rib, then cast (bind) off using a stretchy cast (bind) off.

Project notes

Because of the pattern repeat and tension/ gauge, note that the sizes differ slightly from the recipes – make sure to check the sizing to determine which size will best fit your foot. The toe-up recipe uses a similar toe as these socks (see Sock recipes: Toe-up socks). If you need a refresher for how to use a crochet hook to add beads, see Sock techniques: Adding beads.

Special abbreviation

B, add bead to next stitch using crochet hook, then knit this stitch

Stitch patterns

Bead and lace – sizes XS/S and 2XL (12-stitch repeat)

Round 1: P1, ssk, k4, p3, B, yo, p1.

Round 2: P1, k5, p3, k2, p1.

Round 3: P1, ssk, k3, p3, k1, yo, k1, p1.

Round 4: P1, k4, p3, k3, p1.

Round 5: P1, ssk, k2, p3, B, yo, k2, p1.

Round 6: P1, k3, p3, k4, p1.

Round 7: P1, ssk, k1, p3, k1, yo, k3, p1.

Round 8: P1, k2, p3, k5, p1.

Round 9: P1, ssk, p3, B, yo, k4, p1.

Round 10: P1, k1, p3, k6, p1.

Round 11: P1, yo, B, p3, k4, k2tog, p1.

Round 12: Repeat Round 8.

Round 13: P1, k1, yo, k1, p3, k3, k2tog, p1.

Round 14: Repeat Round 6.

Round 15: P1, k2, yo, B, p3, k2, k2tog, p1.

Round 16: Repeat Round 4.

Round 17: P1, k3, yo, k1, p3, k1, k2tog, p1.

Round 18: Repeat Round 2.

Round 19: P1, k4, yo, B, p3, k2tog, p1.

Round 20: P1, k6, p3, k1, p1.

Key

knit

purl

add bead and knit

k2tog

ssk

yo

Bead and lace – size M (10-stitch repeat)

Round 1: P1, ssk, k4, p1, B, yo, p1.

Round 2: P1, k5, p1, k2, p1.

Round 3: P1, ssk, k3, p1, k1, yo, k1, p1.

Round 4: P1, k4, p1, k3, p1.

Round 5: P1, ssk, k2, p1, B, yo, k2, p1.

Round 6: P1, k3, p1, k4, p1.

Round 7: P1, ssk, k1, p1, k1, yo, k3, p1.

Round 8: P1, k2, p1, k5, p1.

Round 9: P1, ssk, p1, B, yo, k4, p1.

Round 10: P1, k1, p1, k6, p1.

Round 11: P1, yo, B, p1, k4, k2tog, p1.

Round 12: Repeat Round 8.

Round 13: P1, k1, yo, k1, p1, k3, k2tog, p1.

Round 14: Repeat Round 6.

Round 15: P1, k2, yo, B, p1, k2, k2tog, p1.

Round 16: Repeat Round 4.

Round 17: P1, k3, yo, k1, p1, k1, k2tog, p1.

Round 18: Repeat Round 2.

Round 19: P1, k4, yo, B, p1, k2tog, p1.

Round 20: P1, k6, p1, k1, p1.

Bead and lace – size L/XL (11-stitch repeat)

Round 1: P1, ssk, k4, p2, B, yo, p1.

Round 2: P1, k5, p2, k2, p1.

Round 3: P1, ssk, k3, p2, k1, yo, k1, p1.

Round 4: P1, k4, p2, k3, p1.

Round 5: P1, ssk, k2, p2, B, yo, k2, p1.

Round 6: P1, k3, p2, k4, p1.

Round 7: P1, ssk, k1, p2, k1, yo, k3, p1.

Round 8: P1, k2, p2, k5, p1.

Round 9: P1, ssk, p2, B, yo, k4, p1.

Round 10: P1, k1, p2, k6, p1.

Round 11: P1, yo, B, p2, k4, k2tog, p1.

Round 12: Repeat Round 8.

Round 13: P1, k1, yo, k1, p2, k3, k2tog, p1.

Round 14: Repeat Round 6.

Round 15: P1, k2, yo, B, p2, k2, k2tog, p1.

Round 16: Repeat Round 4.

Round 17: P1, k3, yo, k1, p2, k1, k2tog, p1.

Round 18: Repeat Round 2.

Round 19: P1, k4, yo, B, p2, k2tog, p1.

Round 20: P1, k6, p2, k1, p1.

Instructions

Toe

With 2.5mm (US2 or US1) needles, cast on 20 [24] [30] [32] sts using a closed cast on method such as Judy's magic cast on (see Sock techniques: Casting on). Place a stitch marker after stitch 10 [12] [15] [16] and in last st of the round, moving markers up as you work.

Round 1: Knit to end of round.

Round 2: (K1, M1L, knit to last st before marker, M1L, k1) twice. (4 sts increased)

Repeat Rounds 1-2 until there are 48 [60] [66] [72] sts.

Foot

Make sure to use the correct written instructions or chart for your size. Sizes XS/S and 2XL use a 12-stitch repeat, size M uses a 10-stitch repeat, and size L/XL uses an 11-stitch repeat.

Round 1: Working from chart or written instructions for your size, work Round 1 of Bead and lace pattern, repeating 2 [3] [3] [3] times to marker, slip marker, knit to end of round.

Round 2: Work Round 2 of Bead and lace pattern to marker, slip marker, knit to end of round.

These 2 rounds set the pattern on the instep (top of foot) and stocking (stockinette) stitch on the sole (bottom of foot).

Continue in patterns as set until sock measures 9 [10.5] [11.5] [12]cm (3½ [4¼] [4½] [4¾]in) less than the desired foot length (see All about

socks: Choosing the correct size), ending after an even-numbered round of the Bead and lace pattern.

Gusset shaping

Continue to work Bead and lace pattern on the instep and increase for the gusset as instructed on the sole.

Round 1: Work Bead and lace pattern to marker, slip marker, k1, M1L, knit to last st of round, M1R, k1. (2 sts increased)

Round 2: Work Bead and lace pattern to marker, slip marker, knit to end of round.

Repeat Rounds 1-2 until you have 48 [60] [67] [72] sts on sole. (72 [90] [100] [108] total sts)

Make note of which round of Bead and lace pattern you have ended as you need this when working the leg.

Heel turn

The heel turn is worked using double stitch short rows (see Sock techniques: Short rows).

Turn work to begin the heel turn on a WS row.

Row 1 (WS): P36 [45] [50] [54], turn, leaving 12 [15] [17] [18] gusset sts unworked.

Row 2: MDS, k23 [29] [32] [35], turn, leaving 12 [15] [17] [18] gusset sts unworked.

Row 3: MDS, purl to previous DS, turn.

Row 4: MDS, knit to previous DS, turn.

Rows 5-16: Repeat Rows 3-4 six times.

Row 17: MDS, purl to first DS, purl next 7 DS, p2tog (next DS and next plain st), turn, leaving 11 [14] [16] [17] gusset sts unworked.

Row 18: Sl1 wyib, knit to first DS, knit next 7 DS, k2tog (next DS and next plain st), turn, leaving 11 [14] [16] [17] gusset sts unworked.

Heel flap

At the end of each heel flap row, you will be decreasing gusset sts.

Row 1 (WS): Sl1 wyif, p22 [28] [32] [34], p2tog, turn. (1 st decreased)

Row 2: Sl1 wyib, (k1, sl1 wyib) 11 [14] [16] [17] times, k2togtbl, turn. (1 st decreased)

Repeat Rows 1-2 until all gusset sts at each side are worked, ending last row with k2tog [k2tog] [k3tog] [k2tog] to end with 24 [30] [33] [36] sts on sole. Do not turn after final row. (48 [60] [66] [72] total sts)

Leg

Begin working in the round again.

Next round: Starting from the next round in pattern as noted at end of foot, work Bead and lace pattern for your size 4 [6] [6] [6] times around.

Continue in pattern until leg measures 3cm (1⅛in) less than desired length.

Cuff

Rib round: (K1, p1) to end of round.

Work in rib for 3cm (1⅛in).

Cast off all sts using a stretchy cast off, such as Jeny's surprisingly stretchy cast (bind) off (see Sock techniques: Casting (binding) off).

To finish

Weave in all ends and trim. Block your socks and leave to dry completely (see Sock techniques: Finishing your project).

Winter Snow

BY KERSTIN BALKE

With stunning use of colour, these cuff-down socks are a delight with stripes and stranded colourwork. Featuring a boomerang heel to maintain the colour continuity, this pair will show off your growing sock skills in style.

You will need

Yarn
4 colours of yarn are needed:

Lang Yarns Jawoll; 75% virgin wool, 25% nylon/polyamide; 210m (230 yards) per 50g (1.75oz) skein

1 skein each in Beige 226 (Yarn A), Petrol 288 (Yarn B), Fuchsia 366 (Yarn C) and Pink 119 (Yarn D)

This yarn is a 4ply (fingering) weight yarn, so any similar weight yarn would work well (see Checking your tension/ gauge: Substituting yarn).

Needles
2.5mm (US2 or US1) needles for your preferred method of knitting in the round

If using a short circular needle, you will also need a set of DPNs in the same size for the cast on, heels and toes

Extras
Tape measure or ruler; stitch markers; stitch holder (optional); tapestry/yarn needle (for weaving in ends); pair of sock blockers (optional), towel and wool wash for blocking (see Tools and materials: Extras)

Tension/Gauge
36 sts and 41 rows to 10 x 10cm (4 x 4in) measured in pattern using 2.5mm (US2 or US1) needles

If you need to use a different needle size to achieve this tension/gauge, make sure to use that needle size throughout (see Checking your tension/gauge).

Sizes
XS [S] [M] [L] [XL]

Knitted sock, actual knitted circumference:
17.5 [19] [20] [21.5] [22.5]cm (7 [7½] [8] [8½] [8¾]in)

Will stretch to fit approximate foot circumference:
18.5 [20] [21] [22.5] [23.5]cm (7¼ [8] [8¼] [8¾] [9¼]in)

Construction

Cuff-down: these socks are cast on at the cuff and worked in the round to the heel. The **cuff** is a 1 x 1 rib and the **leg** is worked in stranded colourwork, stripes and charted colourwork in alternating sets of 2 colours at a time.

Boomerang heel: the heel is worked in short rows as a **double stitch short row heel** (see Sock elements: Heels) on half the sts for the first part of the heel, then 2 'boomerang' rounds are worked, then further short rows are worked on half the sts for the second half of the heel.

Foot: the **foot** is then worked in rounds with further charted colourwork and stripes in alternating sets of 2 colours at a time.

Toe: the **toe** is shaped with gradual banded decrease rounds, then more frequent decreases until only a few sts are left. The remaining stitches are **threaded through and gathered** to close.

Project notes

Because of the pattern repeat and tension/ gauge, note that the sizes differ slightly from the recipes – make sure to check the sizing to determine which size will best fit your foot.

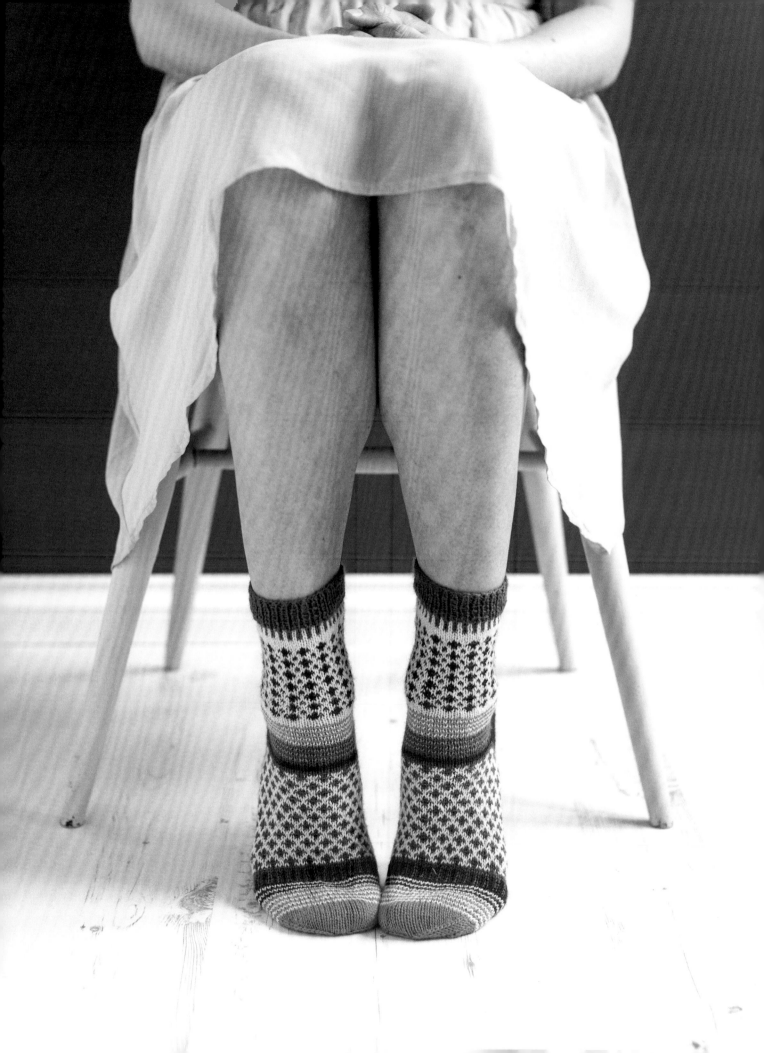

Cuff

With Yarn B, loosely cast on 64 [68] [72] [76] [80] sts onto 1 DPN.

Rib round: (K1, p1) to the end. Do not turn your work (keep the RS of knitting facing you).

Next, starting from the opposite end of the DPN to the working yarn, carefully slip the stitches purlwise onto a short circular needle (or spread your stitches evenly over 4 DPNs), keeping RS of work facing at all times. Join to start knitting in the round (see Knitting in the round: Joining the round). Place a stitch marker in the first or last stitch of the round, moving it up as you work.

Continue in rib pattern (repeating Rib round) until you have worked 12 rounds or desired length.

Leg chart

4
3
2
1

4 3 2 1

Foot chart

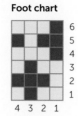

6
5
4
3
2
1

4 3 2 1

Key

☐ Yarn A
■ Yarn B
■ Yarn C

Leg

Join in Yarn A.

Throughout, carry your unused yarn along the inside of the sock and work in stranded colourwork (see Sock techniques: Working with more than one yarn/colour), cutting and joining colours as instructed.

Rounds 1-4: (K1 with Yarn B, k1 with Yarn A) to end of round.

Cut Yarn B.

Rounds 5-7: Using Yarn A, knit 3 rounds.

Join in Yarn C.

Round 8: Using Yarn A and Yarn C, (work Round 1 of Leg chart) to end of round.

Rounds 9-34: Continue in pattern as set, ending after a Round 3 of Leg chart.

Cut Yarn C.

Rounds 35-37: Using Yarn A, knit 3 rounds.

Join in Yarn D.

Round 38: Using Yarn D, knit to end of round.

Round 39: Using Yarn A, knit to end of round.

Rounds 40-45: Repeat Rounds 38-39 three times.

Cut Yarn A and join in Yarn B.

Round 46: Using Yarn D, knit to end of round.

Round 47: Using Yarn B, knit to end of round.

Rounds 48-53: Repeat Rounds 46-47 three times.

Round 54: Repeat Round 47 once more.

Cut Yarn B and Yarn D, and join in Yarn C.

First half of heel

The heel is worked on the next 32 [34] [36] [38] [40] sts using Yarn C only.

Row 1 (RS): K32 [34] [36] [38] [40], turn.

Row 2: MDS, p31 [33] [35] [37] [39], turn.

Row 3: MDS, knit to previous DS, turn.

Row 4: MDS, purl to previous DS, turn.

Repeat Rows 3-4 until 12 sts remain unworked in the middle of the heel, between the DS sts.

Boomerang rounds

Knit 2 rounds on all sts, making sure to work both legs of each DS together as a single st, ending at start of round marker.

Second half of heel

Row 1 (RS): K23 [24] [25] [26] [27], turn.

Row 2: MDS, p13, turn.

Row 3: MDS, knit to previous DS, knit DS, k1, turn.

Row 4: MDS, purl to previous DS, purl DS, p1, turn.

Repeat Rows 3-4 until the final row ends at the start of round marker.

Cut Yarn C.

Foot

Continue working in the round on all sts, making sure to work any remaining DS as single sts when you come to them.

Join in Yarn B.

Using Yarn B, knit 2 rounds.

Join in Yarn A.

Next round: Using Yarn A and Yarn B, (work Round 1 of Foot chart) to end of round.

Continue in pattern as set until sock measures approximately 7.5 [7.5] [8] [8] [8.5]cm (3 [3] [3¼] [3¼] [3½]in) less than desired foot length (see All about socks: Choosing the correct size), ending after a Round 3 of Foot chart.

Cut Yarn A.

Rounds 1-2: Using Yarn B, knit to end of round.

Join in Yarn C.

Rounds 3-6: (K1 with Yarn C, k1 with Yarn B) to end of round.

Cut Yarn B and join in Yarn A.

Round 7: Using Yarn C, knit to end of round.

Round 8: Using Yarn A, knit to end of round.

Rounds 9-12: Repeat Rounds 7-8 twice.

Cut Yarn C and join in Yarn D.

Round 13: Using Yarn D, knit to end of round.

Round 14: Using Yarn A, knit to end of round.

Rounds 15-20: Repeat Rounds 13-14 three times.

Cut Yarn A and complete toe using Yarn D.

If needed, work in stocking (stockinette) stitch until sock measures 2.5 [2.5] [3] [3] [3.5]cm (1 [1] [1¼] [1¼] [1½]in) less than desired length.

Toe

Set-up round: K32 [34] [36] [38] [40], place marker, knit to end of round.

Round 1: *K1, ssk, knit to 3 sts before next marker, k2tog, k1; repeat from * once more. (4 sts decreased)

Rounds 2-3: Knit to end of round, slipping markers.

Round 4: Repeat Round 1.

Round 5: Knit to end of round, slipping markers.

Rounds 6-7: Repeat Rounds 4-5.

Round 9: Repeat Round 1.

Repeat Round 9 until 8 [10] [8] [10] [8] sts remain.

To finish

Cut yarn, leaving a long tail end and thread this end onto a tapestry/yarn needle. Thread through the remaining sts and pull tightly to gather up the hole. Secure the gathers with a few small stitches and weave in end on WS. Weave in any remaining ends and trim. Block your socks and leave to dry completely (see Sock techniques: Finishing your project).

KNITTING IN THE ROUND

Circular knitting, or knitting in the round, is a term used to describe a method of knitting that creates a seamless fabric. The method can be worked with a set of 4 or 5 double-pointed needles (DPNs), short circular needles, long circular needles or flexible short needles.

While some knitters may already be comfortable knitting in the round on one type of needle, other knitters may be more used to knitting flat with 2 needles and may even believe knitting in the round to be quite daunting. But please don't be intimidated to try something new, as it can be really exciting and rewarding.

This chapter takes you through the steps for using each type of needle in the round, so you can try them all out and see which you prefer, or which method feels most comfortable for you.

ON DOUBLE-POINTED NEEDLES (DPNS)

Double-pointed needles, or DPNs, are usually available in sets of 4 or 5, and are a really good starting point for knitting in the round. For socks, I would recommend a set of 5 DPNs so that you can spread your stitches evenly over 4 of the DPNs (with the same number of stitches on each needle) and start knitting with the fifth DPN.

You can knit either cuff-down or toe-up socks with DPNs, from start to finish, without needing any other needles.

To make things much easier, it is better to cast all your stitches onto 1 DPN and knit the first round before joining. Otherwise, if you try to cast on your stitches over 4 DPNs they twist and turn around, and it's very frustrating and fiddly and can be difficult to get started and even completely off-putting. Knitting 1 round before joining will make your stitches easier to manoeuvre around your needles.

1. Cast on the required number of stitches for your sock size onto 1 DPN.

2. Knit the first round of your chosen rib pattern onto a second DPN and don't turn your work at the end (keep the right side facing you).

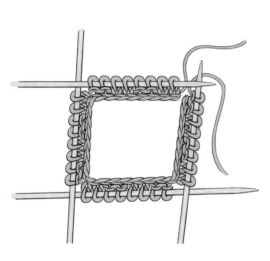

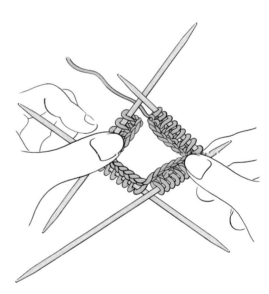

3. Slip the stitches evenly between 4 DPNs (or if you are using a set of 4, then you will need to spread your stitches over 3 DPNs with the fourth as your working needle).

4. Starting at the right-hand side of the DPN (at the opposite end to the working yarn), and keeping right side facing at all times, slide the first 14 [15] [16] [17] [18] sts onto 1 DPN (this is called Needle 4); slide the next 14 [15] [16] [17] [18] sts onto the next DPN (this is called Needle 3); slide the next 14 [15] [16] [17] [18] sts onto the next DPN (this is called Needle 2) and leave the final 14 [15] [16] [17] [18] sts on the original DPN (this is now called Needle 1).

5. Now you will prepare to start knitting in the round. Keeping right side facing, carefully bring the tips of Needle 4 and Needle 1 around together and slide the stitches up to the top of the needles so they are ready to be knitted and join to start working in the round.

Note: *If your stitches are spread over 4 DPNs, they will form a square shape (as shown); if your stitches are spread over 3 DPNs, they will form a triangle shape.*

6. Now you can do one of two things:

Either: just continue with the steps below to start knitting which will leave a small gap between the first and last stitches (don't worry about this because you can use your tail end of yarn to catch this gap together at the end of your knitting when weaving in ends).

Or: avoid the small gap by crossing over the first and last stitches of the round (see Joining the round).

7. Whichever you choose, it will be helpful to use a stitch marker (or your tail end of yarn) to mark the end of the round, but you may wish to place the stitch marker into the first or last stitch of the round, rather than on your DPN, as it will slide off the end.

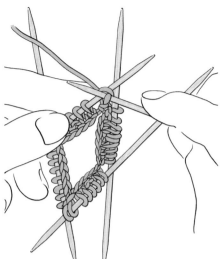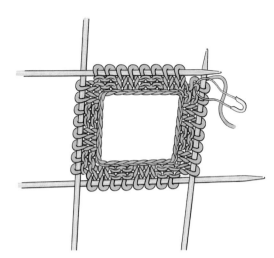

8. With your spare DPN, using the working yarn, hold Needle 1 in your left hand and start knitting off the stitches from Needle 1. Hold Needle 1 in your left hand as you would normally hold your knitting needle, and ignore the rest of the DPNs.

9. When Needle 1 is empty, use this spare DPN to knit off the stitches from Needle 2, and so on with Needles 3 and 4. Use each needle, when it becomes free, as the working needle in turn until you have knitted off all the stitches and the round is complete.

As you move from needle to needle, make sure that you tug your yarn tightly, otherwise the stitches at the ends of your DPNs will be looser and look visibly different.

10. If you are using a stitch marker between stitches, simply slip this at the start of each round. If you are using the tail end of yarn or a removable stitch marker in the first or last stitch, move it up after a few rounds.

JOINING THE ROUND

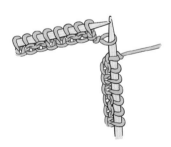

1. Insert the tip of the right-hand needle *purlwise* into the top stitch on left-hand needle.

2. Slide it off the left-hand needle and onto right-hand needle.

3. Insert the tip of left-hand needle *purlwise* into the second stitch on right-hand needle, lift this stitch up and over the top stitch and onto left-hand needle.

4. The stitches are now crossed and the top stitch on left-hand needle is now the first stitch of the round.

ON A SHORT CIRCULAR NEEDLE

These are specially designed for sock knitting because the flexible cable in between the needle tips is short enough so that when your sock stitches are on the needles, the cable will bend and the needle tips will meet so that you can knit without stretching your stitches.

Some short circular needles have one tip longer than the other, which is useful for holding and it creates less stress on your hand. The shorter needle tip is good for knitting with but if you prefer you can knit with the longer needle tip too – it's really down to personal choice.

If you are using a short circular for cuff-down socks, it is easier to cast on using a spare DPN of the same size, since it's much easier to hold a straight DPN than a flexible needle for knitting off your stitches onto the short circulars.

1. Cast on the required number of stitches for your sock size onto 1 DPN. Knit the first round of your rib pattern onto the short circular and don't turn your work at the end.

2. Spread your stitches around the cable and needle tips and bring the needle tips together.

It is essential that all of your stitches have the right side facing you; don't let any stitches twist around the needles otherwise your knitting will have a twist in it too.

3. The first stitch on the left-hand needle tip is the first stitch of the round and the top stitch on the right-hand needle tip is the last stitch of the round.

4. Now you can do one of two things:

Either: just continue with the steps below to start knitting which will leave a small gap between the first and last stitches (don't worry about this because you can use your tail end of yarn to catch this gap together at the end of your knitting when weaving in ends).

Or: avoid the small gap by crossing over the first and last stitches of the round (see Joining the round).

5. Whichever you choose, it will be helpful to use a stitch marker (or your tail end of yarn) to mark the start of the round.

6. Start knitting your stitches according to your pattern, moving them around the short circular needle as you knit. If you are using a stitch marker, you simply slip this at the start of each round or move up your tail end of yarn after a few rounds.

Note: *For toe-up socks, you can switch to short circulars once you have knitted the toe section and are ready to start knitting the foot.*

ON A LONG CIRCULAR NEEDLE FOR MAGIC LOOP

This method of knitting in the round allows you to use a long circular needle to knit a small number of stitches in the round, which is really ingenious.

You may prefer this method if your hands ache with short circulars, or you may find that DPNs are just too fiddly and are looking for a different method.

Magic loop is very similar to knitting with straight needles and much less stressful on the hands. You can also divide the top and bottom stitches of your socks evenly over the 2 needle tips, which really helps with knitting and counting, as the sock elements are much easier to identify.

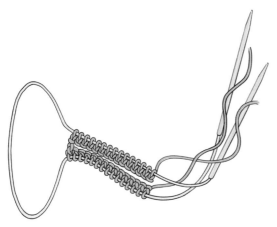

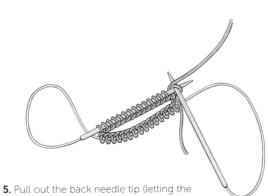

1. Using you preferred cast on method (see Sock techniques: Casting on), cast on the required number of stitches for your chosen size onto 1 needle tip of your circular needle.

2. Slide these stitches off the needle tip and onto the cable.

3. Locate the halfway point of your stitches and pull the cable through between the 2 sets of stitches, folding it as you pull it through. Your 2 sets of stitches are now sitting on each side of the folded cable.

4. Slide these sets of stitches off the cable and onto the needle tips.

5. Pull out the back needle tip (letting the back stitches slide onto the cable again) and use this free needle tip to knit off the stitches from the front needle tip. Make sure that you pull the yarn tightly before you start knitting.

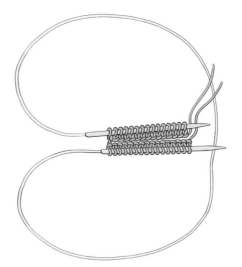

6. Slide both sets of stitches back onto the needle tips again.

7. Repeat **Step 5**, then **Step 6**, to knit the other half of your stitches. You have now completed 1 round.

Repeat **Steps 5 and 6** twice for each round of knitting.

ON FLEXIBLE SHORT NEEDLES

These sets of 3 needles are relatively new to the world of sock knitting, and are a great alternative to magic loop. They are a sort of hybrid of a short circular and a DPN, with a very short, flexible cable in the centre of 2 needle tips. You use them in exactly the same way as magic loop knitting, but you have a third needle to knit with.

 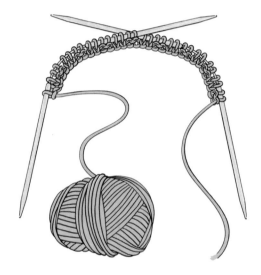

1. Using you preferred cast on method (see Sock techniques: Casting on), cast on the required number of stitches for your chosen size onto 1 needle.

2. Using one of the spare needles, work your first row of knitting as per your pattern. Do not turn your work.

3. Divide the stitches between 2 needles by working from right-hand side of needle (from opposite end to working yarn), slipping the first half of stitches onto a new needle.

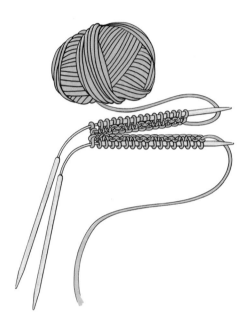

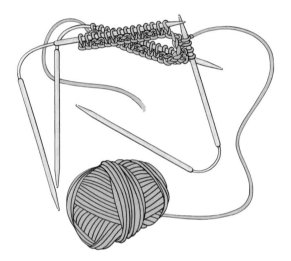

4. Bring original needle to sit behind the new needle. Working yarn is on first stitch of back needle and the wrong side is facing inwards.

5. Use the spare needle to knit off the stitches from the front needle. Make sure that you pull the yarn tightly before you start knitting.

6. Rotate needles so that they are pointing in the right direction for knitting, with yarn located on back needle again. If needed, move stitches on front needle towards the tip.

Repeat **Step 5** to knit off the second half of your stitches then repeat **Step 6**. You have now completed 1 round.

Don't worry about the small gap at the start of the round as you can close this at the end of your knitting by joining it up with your tail end of yarn with a few stitches when weaving in ends.

Repeat **Steps 5 and 6** twice for each round of knitting.

TWO AT A TIME MAGIC LOOP KNITTING

While it may seem daunting, this method is based on the regular magic loop method for knitting one sock at a time, so if you have tried that method and enjoy it, then this could be the next step for you.

The benefit of knitting 2 socks together is that their pattern repeats will match and both socks will be finished at the same time.

Working cuff-down

BEFORE YOU BEGIN

Split your ball or skein of yarn into 2 equal balls (or use 2 separate full balls). If your yarn is striped or has a notable pattern sequence, you may want to make sure that both your balls start at the same point in the yarn's pattern and that you make your slip knot at the same point on each ball. That way your socks will match as perfectly as possible (noting that some repeat sequences may be slightly different from others so they may not match exactly).

CASTING ON TWO AT A TIME FOR CUFF-DOWN SOCKS

1. Make sure to use the long-tail cast on (thumb method) (see Sock techniques: Casting on). For the first set of sock stitches (Sock 1), cast on *half* of your required number of stitches from the first ball of yarn.

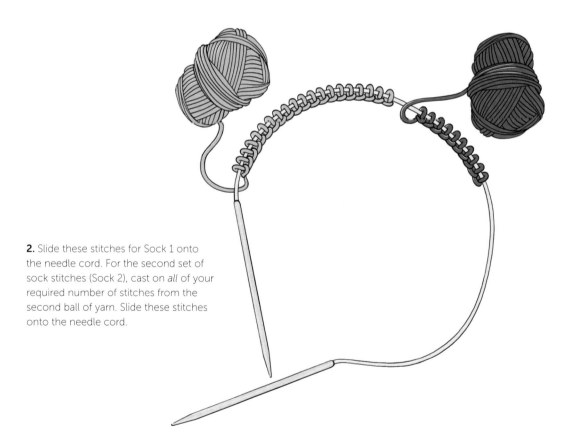

2. Slide these stitches for Sock 1 onto the needle cord. For the second set of sock stitches (Sock 2), cast on *all* of your required number of stitches from the second ball of yarn. Slide these stitches onto the needle cord.

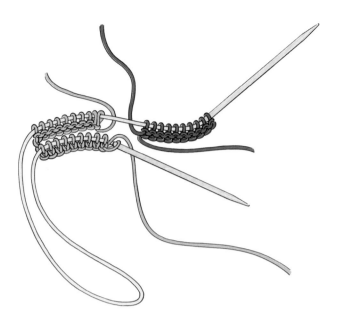

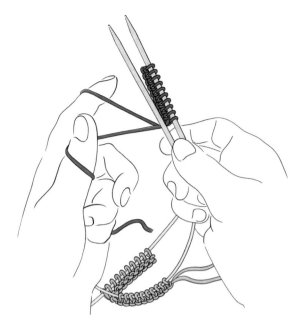

3. Locate the halfway point of stitches for Sock 2 and pull the cable through between the 2 halves, folding it as you pull it through. The stitches for Sock 2 are now split in half and are sitting on each side of the folded cable. Stitches for Sock 1 are now sitting above Sock 2, on the back cord.

4. Slide stitches for Sock 1 onto the back needle tip.

5. Flip the needle tips so that stitches for Sock 1 are positioned to the right of the empty needle tip. The yarn from the ball will be at the base of these stitches.

6. Using long-tail cast on (thumb method) again, cast on the other half of stitches for Sock 1 and leave these stitches on the needle tips. The stitches for Sock 1 are now split over the needle tips and the Sock 2 stitches are sitting on the cord, separated at the halfway point by the cord. Each sock has its own ball of yarn attached.

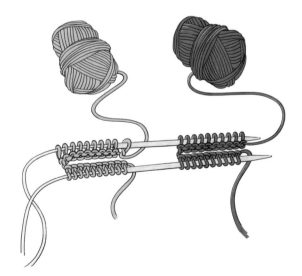

7. Push Sock 2 stitches right up to the base of the needle tips so that the folded cord is as long as it can be.

TO START KNITTING TWO AT A TIME

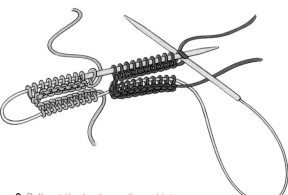

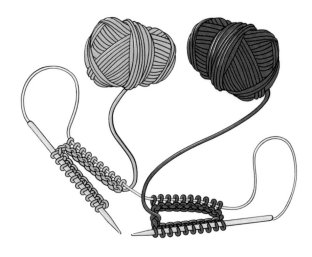

8. Pull out the back needle and let the back stitches of Sock 1 slide onto the cord, but take care not to pull the cord out too much otherwise you may pull out the cord from in between the stitches of Sock 2.

9. Use this free needle to knit off the stitches from front needle, using yarn for Sock 1. Make sure that you pull the yarn tightly before you start knitting. Knit across the Sock 1 stitches, drop yarn.

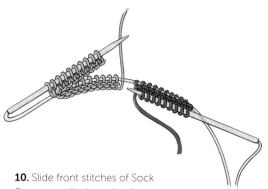

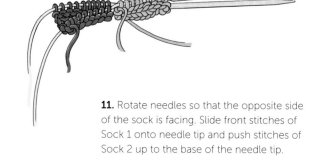

10. Slide front stitches of Sock 2 onto needle tip and, using yarn for Sock 2, knit off the stitches from front needle.

11. Rotate needles so that the opposite side of the sock is facing. Slide front stitches of Sock 1 onto needle tip and push stitches of Sock 2 up to the base of the needle tip.

12. Repeat **Steps 8-11** to knit the other half of your stitches for each sock.

You have now completed 1 round.

Repeat **Steps 8-11** twice for each round of knitting.

Working toe-up

1. Cast on using Judy's magic cast on (see Sock techniques: Casting on) for Sock 1, which leaves the stitches sitting on both needle tips. Push these stitches along the needle, but not too far.

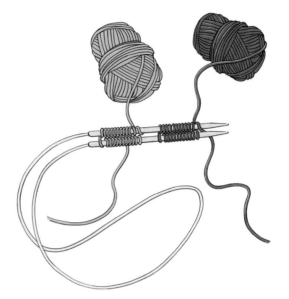

2. Cast on the stitches for Sock 2 onto the now-free needle tips. Both socks are on the needles and ready to knit.

Work as Working cuff-down from **Step 8** to begin knitting in the round.

SOCK TECHNIQUES

Here you will find illustrated guides to help you with all of the techniques needed for knitting the sock recipes and projects in this book, such as colourwork and short rows, so that you can start with the basics and move on to more challenging socks, as and when you're ready.

You may find it useful to also go through the Sock recipes section, which has photo step-by-step guides for cuff-down, toe-up and two-needle socks.

Even if you're an established knitter, you may find a few new techniques to try, or different ways of knitting.

CASTING ON

Long-tail cast on (thumb method)

This makes a firm and neat cast-on edge which is also stretchy and perfect for socks.

1. Pull a length of yarn from the ball, just over 3 times the measurement of your leg circumference. Make a slip knot at this point and place it on your needle. Hold the needle in your right hand.

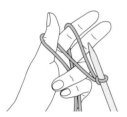 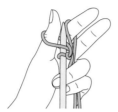 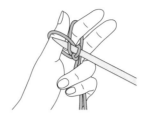 

2. With your free hand, grab the yarn from the ball together with the tail end of yarn and insert your thumb and first finger in between the 2 strands. Keep the yarn from the ball over your thumb and the tail end over your first finger.

3. Bring your thumb towards you and take it under the front strand to form a loop around your thumb.

4. Tilt needle forwards and to the right and over, then under and up through the front strand of the loop around your thumb (from bottom to top).

5. Tilt needle upwards and slightly to the left and over, then under, the top strand from your first finger.

6. Draw it through the loop from your thumb and let the loop slide off your thumb and make a new stitch on the needle.

7. Form a new loop around your thumb.

Repeat **Steps 4-7** until you have the required number of stitches.

German twisted cast on

1. Start with a slip knot on the needle, then hold the yarn as for Steps 1-3 of the Long-tail cast on (thumb method) in a slingshot shape with yarn over the index finger and thumb of your left hand.

  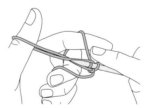 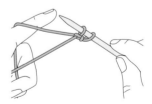

2. Bring the needle under both strands on your thumb, then dip the needle down into the centre of the loop on your thumb, catching the side of the thumb yarn further from you and twisting it up and towards you.

3. Next move the needle into the loop on your finger and catching the strand between finger and thumb.

4. Bring the needle with the yarn through the small gap in the twisted loop on your thumb.

5. Let go of the loop on your thumb and tighten the stitch onto the needle.

6. Position the strands over your thumb and index finger again.

Repeat **Steps 2-6** until you have the required number of stitches.

Cable cast on (two-needle cast on)

1. Leave a 10-15cm (4-6in) tail end of yarn and make a slip knot onto 1 needle which counts as your first stitch. Hold this needle in your left hand. Insert the right-hand needle into the slip knot.

2. Knit into the slip knot as you would a regular knit stitch (see Basic stitches – Knit stitch), but do not take it off the left-hand needle.

3. Transfer the loop from the right-hand needle to the left-hand needle by inserting the left-hand needle up through the bottom of the loop, and tighten the stitch if needed by pulling the working yarn.

4. Insert your right-hand needle in between the top 2 stitches on left-hand needle.

5. Take yarn around the back needle (as if to knit) and pull a loop through to the front of work.

Repeat **Steps 3-5** until you have the required number of stitches.

Alternating cable cast on

This makes a neat edge for 1 x 1 ribbed knitting and is great for socks.

1. Leave a 10-15cm (4-6in) tail end of yarn and make a slip knot onto 1 needle which counts as your first stitch. Hold this needle in your left hand.

2. Insert the right-hand needle into the slip knot and knit as you would a regular knit stitch (see Basic stitches – Knit stitch), but do not take it off the left-hand needle.

3. Transfer the loop from the right-hand needle to the left-hand needle by inserting the left-hand needle up through the bottom of the loop.

4. The next stitch is made *purlwise*; insert your right-hand needle between the last 2 stitches from back to front. Wrap the yarn around the right-hand needle tip and draw it through to the back.

5. Transfer the loop from the right-hand needle to the left-hand needle by inserting the left-hand needle up through the bottom of the loop.

6. The next stitch is made *knitwise*; insert your right-hand needle between the last 2 stitches from front to back. Wrap the yarn around the right-hand needle tip and draw it through to the front.

Repeat **Steps 3-6** until you have made the number of stitches required and alternating between the knit and purl stitches.

Judy's magic cast on (by Judy Becker)

1. Make a slip knot, leaving a long tail end of yarn of approximately 30cm (12in). Place the slip knot onto 1 of the needles, which counts as your first stitch. Then hold 2 needles in your right hand, alongside each another, with the slip knot on the top needle and the yarn ends sitting behind the bottom needle.

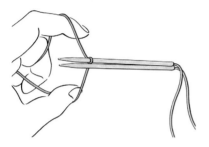
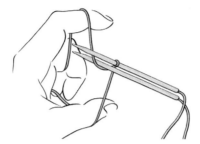
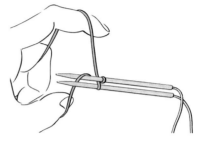

2. Grab the yarn ends in the palm of your left hand – and insert your first finger and thumb in between the strands of yarn to separate them, with the tail end of yarn over your first finger and the yarn from the ball over your thumb.

3. Using your right hand to create a figure-of-eight motion, tilt the tip of the bottom needle upwards to the right and take it over, and then under the strand of yarn from your index finger. This will wrap the yarn around the front needle. The yarn is now located at the back, between the 2 needles and you now have 1 new stitch on each needle.

4. Next, take the tip of the back needle downwards and to the left and over, and then under the working end of yarn which will wrap the yarn around the back needle. The yarn is once again located at the back, between the 2 needles.

This motion also twists the yarn strands so that the stitches become connected and there is no gap between the top and bottom stitches.

5. Repeat **Step 3** to cast on another stitch onto the bottom needle (you now have 2 stitches on each needle).

6. Repeat **Steps 4 and 5** for as many stitches as you need for your chosen size, making sure that you finish when you have the same number of stitches on each needle.

Note: The top yarn strand always wraps around the bottom needle, and the bottom yarn strand always wraps around the top needle.

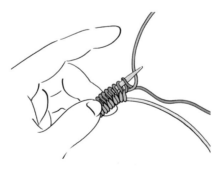

7. Rotate the needles so that they are pointing in the correct direction, ready to knit. There is a small row of purl bumps which should sit on the back of the stitches and this is the wrong side of your knitting. Pull out the bottom needle and use this as your working needle to begin knitting the stitches off the top (now left-hand) needle.

BASIC STITCHES

Knit stitch

  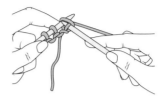 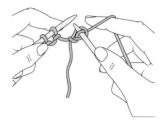

1. Hold needle with stitches to be knitted in your left hand with yarn behind the work. Insert right-hand needle into first stitch on left-hand needle from front to back, with right-hand needle sitting underneath left-hand needle.

2. Take the yarn around the back needle anti-clockwise (counter-clockwise), to form a loop.

3. Bring right-hand needle and the new loop through the stitch to front of your work.

4. Slide the original stitch off the left-hand needle. One knit stitch is now sitting on the right-hand needle.

Purl stitch

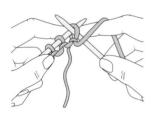 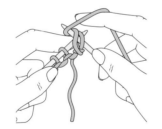 

1. Hold needle with stitches to be purled in your left hand, with yarn at front of the work. Insert right-hand needle through front of first stitch, from right to left with right-hand needle sitting on top of left-hand needle.

2. Take the yarn around the front needle anti-clockwise (counter-clockwise), to form a loop.

3. Bring the right-hand needle and the new loop through the stitch and to the back of your work.

4. Slide the original stitch off left-hand needle. One purl stitch is now sitting on the right-hand needle.

Slip stitch

SLIP STITCH PURLWISE

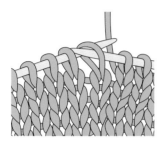

1. To slip a stitch *purlwise*, insert the right-hand needle through the stitch on the left-hand needle from right to left.

2. The slipped stitch will not be twisted on right-hand needle.

SLIP STITCH KNITWISE

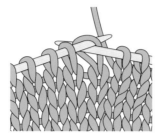

1. To slip a stitch *knitwise*, insert the right-hand needle through the stitch from left to right.

2. The slipped stitch will be twisted on right-hand needle.

If it is not indicated, slip stitches purlwise with yarn held in the back. Otherwise follow the pattern instructions, which may tell you to hold the yarn in the front or the back of the work, as well as whether to work the stitch purlwise or knitwise.

K1tbl (knit 1 through the back leg)

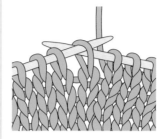

1. Insert right-hand needle into the back leg of the stitch on the left-hand needle.

2. Knit the stitch as you normally would.

Working into the back leg twists the stitch and creates a different texture to a regular stitch.

To work a p1tbl (purl 1 through the back leg), insert the right-hand needle into the back leg of the stitch on the left-hand needle and purl as you normally would.

READING CHARTS

When working colourwork patterns, a chart is usually provided for the pattern, in the form of a grid square. This can be in addition to, or in replacement of, written instructions.

When reading a chart, each grid square on the chart represents 1 stitch and you will knit that stitch in the colour shown on the chart.

Because socks are knitted in the round, you will read every row of the chart from right to left.

For this pattern on Round 1 of your knitting you will read the first row of the chart: 1 stitch is knitted using Yarn A, 1 stitch is knitted using Yarn B, then 2 stitches are knitted using Yarn A.

This 4-stitch pattern is repeated across the same round of knitting, until you reach the end of the round.

For the second round you will read the second row of the chart: 3 sts are knitted in Yarn B, then 1 st in Yarn A.

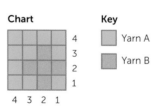

This 4-stitch pattern is repeated across the same round of knitting, until you reach the end of the round.

After a few rounds this will become intuitive, particularly as the knitting will visually resemble the chart.

The same applies to charts with lace or cable patterns. The charts symbols and key will tell you which stitch to knit as a specific colour or using a specific technique.

INCREASING

Kfb (knit front and back)

1. You will be knitting into the front and then the back of the same stitch. First, knit into the front of the next stitch on the left-hand needle without slipping it off the needle.

2. With the stitch still on the left-hand needle, take the tip of the right-hand needle to the back of the work and insert it into the back leg of the same stitch.

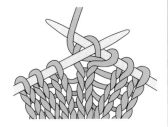

3. Knit the stitch again, through the back leg.

4. Slip the original stitch off the left-hand needle. There are 2 stitches now sitting on the right-hand needle and you have increased by 1 stitch.

Yarn over increases (yo)

A yarn over increase adds a stitch by creating an extra loop of yarn between 2 other stitches. How you create it depends on where the yarn is situated after the last-worked stitch and what stitch comes next.

AFTER A KNIT STITCH

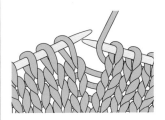

1. Yarn is at back after a knit stitch.

2a. Before working a *knit* stitch, bring yarn to the front in between the needles and over right-hand needle to the back again, ready to knit next stitch.

2b. Before working a *purl* stitch, bring yarn to the front in between the needles, over right-hand needle to the back, then down and between the needles again, ready to purl next stitch.

AFTER A PURL STITCH

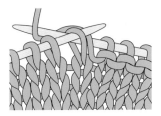

1. Yarn is at front after a purl stitch.

2a. Before working a *knit* stitch, take yarn over the right-hand needle and to back of work ready to knit next stitch.

2b. Before working a *purl* stitch, take yarn over right-hand needle to the back, then between needles to the front again, ready to purl next stitch.

Make 1 stitch

You will make a new stitch by picking up the strand of yarn lying between the 2 needles and knitting into it. The way that you pick up the stitch and knit into it will determine the direction in which it leans.

M1L (MAKE 1 STITCH LEFT-LEANING)

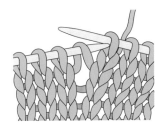 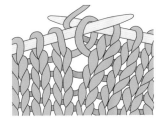

1. Insert the tip of the left-hand needle, from front to the back, beneath the horizontal bar lying between the 2 needles, where you want the increase.

2. Insert tip of right-hand needle into the back leg of this loop and knit the stitch. Knitting into the back leg twists the stitch and avoids making a hole.

M1R (MAKE 1 STITCH RIGHT-LEANING)

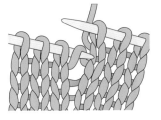 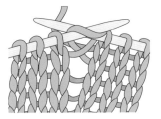

1. Insert the tip of the left-hand needle, from back to the front, beneath the horizontal bar lying between the 2 needles, where you want the increase.

2. Insert tip of right-hand needle into the front leg of this loop and knit the stitch. Knitting into the front leg twists the stitch and avoids making a hole.

DECREASING

Right-leaning decreases

K2TOG

Knit 2 stitches together

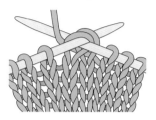

1. Insert right-hand needle through both of the first 2 stitches on the left-hand needle.

2. Knit them together as you would normally for a knit stitch, slipping both stitches off the left-hand needle at the same time.

P2TOG

Purl 2 stitches together

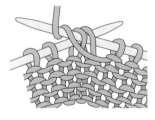

1. Insert right-hand needle through both of the first 2 stitches on the left-hand needle.

2. Purl them together as you would normally for a purl stitch, slipping both stitches off the left-hand needle at the same time.

Left-leaning decreases

SKPO

Slip 1 stitch, knit 1 stitch, pass slipped stitch over

1. Slip the next stitch *knitwise* from left-hand to right-hand needle.

2. Knit the next stitch on the left-hand needle.

3. Insert left-hand needle into the slipped stitch, lift it over the stitch just knitted and take it off the right-hand needle.

> *You can substitute ssk for skpo if you prefer.*

SSK

Slip, slip, knit 2 stitches together

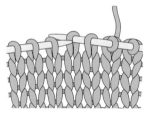 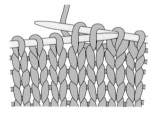

1. Slip next 2 stitches *knitwise* 1 at a time from the left-hand to the right-hand needle.

2. Insert the tip of the left-hand needle from left to right through the front leg of both stitches and knit them together.

> *You can substitute skpo for ssk if you prefer.*

Double decreases

CDD

Centred double decrease – slip 2 stitches together knitwise, knit 1 stitch, pass 2 slipped stitches over

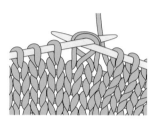

1. Slip next 2 stitches on the left-hand needle together *knitwise*.

2. Knit the next stitch on the left-hand needle.

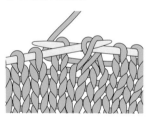

3. Pass the 2 slipped stitches over the knitted stitch.

K3TOG

Knit 3 stitches together

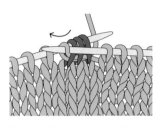

1. Insert right-hand needle through first 3 stitches on the left-hand needle.

2. Knit these together as you would normally for a knit stitch, slipping them all off the left-hand needle at the same time.

SK2PO

Slip 1 stitch, knit 2 stitches together, pass slipped stitch over

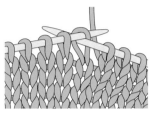

1. Slip next stitch from left-hand needle to right-hand needle.

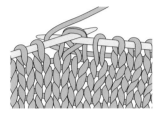

2. Knit next 2 stitches on left-hand needle together.

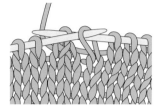

3. Pass the slipped stitch over the k2tog stitch.

ADDING BEADS

Make sure the head of the crochet hook easily fits through your bead.

1. Place bead onto the crochet hook.

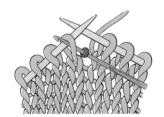

2. Insert the crochet hook into the next stitch on left-hand needle.

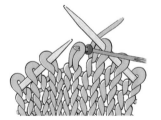

3. Slip the stitch off needle and onto the crochet hook so it sits above the bead.

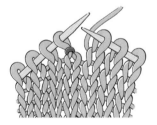

4. Pull the stitch through the bead, so it sits at the base of the stitch and place the stitch on left-hand needle ready to knit.

PICKING UP STITCHES

When picking up along an edge, work 1 full stitch in from the edge (so that 2 loops of yarn are on the tip of the needle). This avoids large holes from forming.

Along edge from right side of work

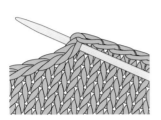 

1. Holding the needle in your right hand insert the needle from the front to the back in the stitch or in the space between stitches.

2. Next wrap the yarn around the needle as if you were working a knit stitch, and then pull the loop on the needle through to the front of your knitting to create a new stitch.

Continue like this until you have the required amount of stitches.

Along edge from wrong side of work

If you need to pick up stitches on the wrong side (purl side) follow the same steps as Along edge from right side of work, but insert needle from the back to the front and wrap the yarn around the needle as if you are working a purl stitch, pulling the loop on the needle to the back of your knitting to create the new stitch.

From waste yarn for forethought heel

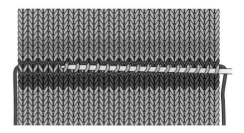

1. With right side of work facing, and working along the stitches directly underneath the waste yarn, use tip of needle to lift the right leg of each stitch onto 1 DPN.

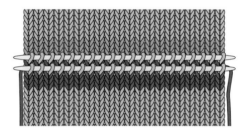

2. Working in the same way to pick up the stitches above the waste yarn, keep right side facing you and rotate the sock, then use tip of needle to lift the right leg of each stitch now underneath the waste yarn onto a second DPN.

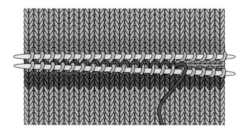

3. Remove the waste yarn by carefully unpicking each loop of waste yarn from the stitches on the DPNs, starting at a tail end of the waste yarn. Make sure to keep the live stitches securely on the DPNs.

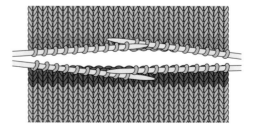

4. Divide your stitches onto 4 DPNs or a circular needle ready to work the heel as instructed.

CABLES

To make a cable, you slip a specified number of stitches onto a cable needle and place the cable needle either at the front or at the back of your work (your pattern will tell you how many and which direction).

This is often written in the form of an abbreviation, like C4F and C4B, T2F or Cr6F. The C, T or Cr before the number tells you if these stitches are regular cables, twisted cables or crossed cables. The number usually tells you how many stitches in total are involved (some patterns may give the number to place on the cable needle – make sure to read the abbreviations with your pattern to be sure). The F or B indicates whether you should hold the stitches to the front (F) or to the back (B) of your work.

This guide shows you how to work a 4-stitch cable leaning to the left (C4F) and a 4-stitch cable leaning to the right (C4B), but the general principle is the same no matter the number of stitches involved in a specific cable. Simply follow the instructions as listed in the abbreviations guide for your pattern.

LEFT-LEANING CABLE WITH 4 STITCHES (C4F)

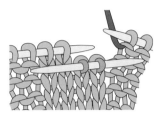

1. Place the next 2 sts onto your cable needle and leave the cable needle at the front of your work.

2. Knit the next 2 sts from the left-hand needle then pick up the cable needle and knit the 2 sts from the cable needle in the same order that they are presented. Your cable is now complete and your sts are crossed and leaning to the left.

RIGHT-LEANING CABLE WITH 4 STITCHES (C4B)

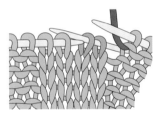

1. Place the next 2 sts onto your cable needle and leave the cable needle at the back of your work.

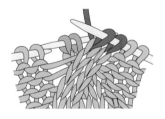

2. Knit the next 2 sts from the left-hand needle then pick up the cable needle and knit the 2 sts from the cable needle in the same order that they are presented. Your cable is now complete and your sts are crossed and leaning to the right.

CROSS CABLE WITH 8 STITCHES (CR8F)

Some cables may involve more stitches, and some will cross stitches in multiple ways and require a second cable needle. This guide shows how to work the Cr8F from the Twisting Pathways socks (see Sock projects). The Cr8B is worked in a similar way.

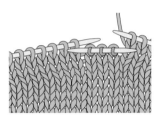

1. Place next 3 sts onto your first cable needle and leave the cable needle at the front of your work.

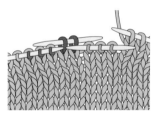

2. Place next 2 sts onto your second cable needle and leave this cable needle at the back of your work.

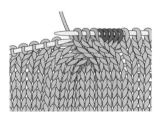

3. Knit the next 3 stitches from the left-hand needle, then purl the 2 stitches from the back cable needle and knit the 3 stitches from the front cable needle to complete the cable.

SHORT ROWS

Wrap and turn (W&T) short rows

The wrap and turn method is a form of short row knitting and it allows you to add extra length or width to a small area of your knitting, therefore forming a neat wedge, or pocket, for your heel.

You will form a small wrap of yarn around the base of a stitch before turning and this avoids a hole being formed.

When you next need to work this stitch, you will pick up the wrap from the base of the stitch and knit or purl it along with the main stitch.

The method I use creates a neat, defined spine along the centre point of the heel, leaving both sides of the heel looking the same.

Note: There are various ways to wrap and turn and you may prefer a different method – you can simply substitute your preferred method if you have one.

W&T ON A PURL ROW

Purl as instructed until you reach the stitch to be wrapped.

1. Take yarn to the back, between needles. Slip next stitch *purlwise* to right-hand needle.

2. Bring yarn forward, between needles.

3. Slip stitch back to left-hand needle.

4. Turn work. Wrap and turn is complete and yarn is at back, ready to knit the next row.

W&T ON A KNIT ROW

Knit as instructed until you reach the stitch to be wrapped.

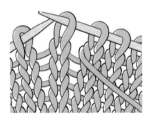 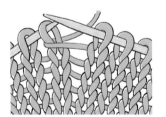

1. Bring yarn forward between needles. With yarn at front, slip next stitch *purlwise* to right-hand needle.

2. Take yarn to the back, between needles. Slip stitch back to left-hand needle

3. Turn work. Wrap and turn is complete and yarn is now at front, ready to purl the next row.

WRAPPED STITCHES

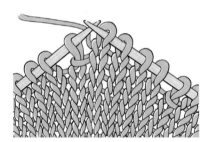

When you have finished your W&T rows, you will see that there are small gaps in between the stitches that are wrapped.

When instructed to knit these wrapped stitches, you will knit them, along with the wraps. This is called 'picking up' the wraps. The method is the same whether you have 1 wrap around your stitch, or 2 wraps and is easier than it sounds and is just like working 2 sts together.

PICKING UP A WRAP ON A KNIT ROW

1. When you reach the wrapped stitch, slip this stitch from left-hand needle *purlwise* to the right-hand needle.

PICKING UP A WRAP ON A PURL ROW

1. When you reach the wrapped stitch, slip this stitch from left-hand needle *purlwise* to the right-hand needle.

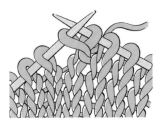

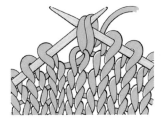

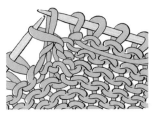

2. Insert the left-hand needle into the front leg of the wrap (or wraps) at the base of the stitch.

3. Slip the original stitch back to the left-hand needle.

4. Knit both the stitch and wrap(s) together through back legs.

2. Insert the left-hand needle into the wrap(s) at the base of the stitch.

3. Slip the wrap(s) onto the right-hand needle and remove left-hand needle from the stitch.

4. Insert left-hand needle into the back of both the stitch and wrap(s) and purl together.

Double stitch short rows (German short rows)

This is another way to work short rows and helps prevent holes. The DS (double stitch) is worked after the turn, where the wrap of the previous method is worked before the turn.

Work as instructed until you reach the point where the work is turned. Turn work as instructed, then MDS (make a double stitch) as follows:

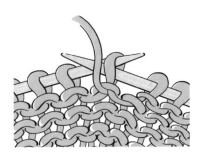

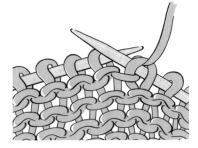

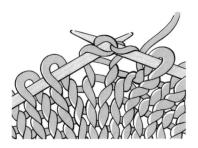

1. Holding yarn in front, slip next stitch on left-hand needle *purlwise*.

2. Pull yarn upwards, over the needle and to the back. Pull firmly on the slipped stitch until it shows 2 legs of the stitch on the needle. This looks like 2 stitches and is why it's called a 'double stitch'.

3. Continue to work in pattern as instructed.

When you are working the following rows/rounds and come to a DS, treat the 2 legs of the stitch as if it's a single stitch. This means that if you would knit that stitch, knit both legs of the stitch together as if you are working a k2tog. If you are purling, work both legs of the double stitch as if for a p2tog.

WORKING WITH MORE THAN ONE YARN/COLOUR

Holding two yarns together at once

You may want to hold 2 strands of yarn together when you are knitting either to get a different effect from the yarns (such as for the Under the Stars sequined socks in Sock projects), or to use 2 thinner yarns to get a thicker yarn – for example 2 strands of 4ply (fingering) equal about a double knitting (DK/8ply) yarn.

This sounds harder than it is. Firstly, no matter how tempting it seems, do not wind the 2 balls of yarn together as 1 ball. Different yarns will pull off the ball at different rates, and will cause you no end of problem with your tension/gauge.

1. Simply hold both strands of yarn in your hand as you would hold a single strand. When you are knitting, simply wind both strands around the needle as normal.

2. When you are working stitches, remember to work each set of double loops as 1 stitch.

Changing colours

Changing between colours in your knitting can be done in a variety of ways. Here are 2 simple ways, with and without a knot.

WITH A LOOSE KNOT

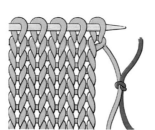

1. To join in a new colour, you can simple tie the new colour around the current colour loosely and push the knot to the top of the current colour.

2. Start knitting with new colour.

WITHOUT A KNOT

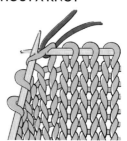

1. Take new colour and. leaving a tail end of about 10-15cm (4-6in), wrap the tail end around the current colour, making a single twist in the yarns. Do this near to the needles.

2. You can tighten up the stitches if needed before you weave in your ends.

Carrying yarn along inside of your work

When you are working in deep stripes in the round, it will depend on how deep your stripes are as to whether it's best to cut yarn at each colour change or to carry the yarn along the inside of your work. This is something you can decide.

To carry yarn along the inside helps you to avoid cutting off the yarn after each stripe, which reduces the need to sew in all the loose ends for every colour change. You will keep both yarn colours attached to the knitting, so it's a good idea to keep your balls of yarn separate and tidy, to avoid tangles.

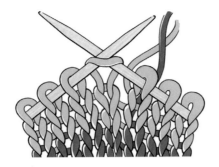

1. When you switch back to a previous colour (that is already attached to your knitting), take the previous colour yarn and wrap it anti-clockwise (counter-clockwise) around the working yarn.

2. Continue knitting with the new colour for 2-4 rounds. Note that if you work too many rounds, the strand of yarn being carried along the inside of your work may snag on your toes when you're putting on your socks.

3. Wrap the previous yarn anti-clockwise (counter-clockwise) again in the same way as before in **Step 1**.

It's important to ensure that you wrap the yarn in the correct direction so that the carried yarn does not show through the knitting, and also to add some elasticity to the fabric.

Jogless stripes

When you knit in the round, you are knitting in a continuous spiral and therefore the end of the round is slightly higher than the beginning of the round, which creates a 'jog' in the stripes. This means that the change of colour is clearly visible where the start and end of the round meet.

You can smooth the jog by using the following method:

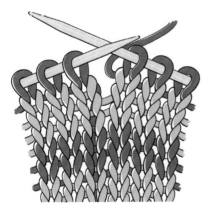

1. After changing colour (see Changing colours), knit 1 full round in the new colour.

2. Before you start the next round, use the right-hand needle to lift the right-hand leg of the stitch that sits below the first stitch on the left-hand needle up and onto the tip of the left-hand needle.

3. Knit these 2 stitches together.

4. This will create an elongated stitch that disguises the jog and keeps your stripes looking neat.

Corrugated rib

Corrugated rib is ribbing that alternates between knit and purl stitches and also between colours. When working in the round, generally the knit stitches are always worked in one colour and the purl stitches in a different colour.

This guide shows you how you would work a 1 x 1 corrugated rib. You can work in other rib patterns in a similar way (such as 3 x 1 or 2 x 2 as in Sock elements: Cuffs).

1. Knit 1 stitch with Yarn A, then leave Yarn A at back.

 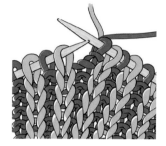 

2. Strand Yarn B across back of work (not too tightly) and bring Yarn B to the front between needles.

3. Purl 1 stitch with Yarn B, then take Yarn B to the back, between needles.

4. Strand Yarn A across back of work (not too tightly).

5. Repeat **Steps 1-4** until the end of the round.

Stranded colourwork and Fair Isle knitting

Some socks use stranded colourwork where 2 (or more) colours of yarn are used in the same round, while repeating a pattern.

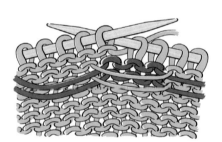 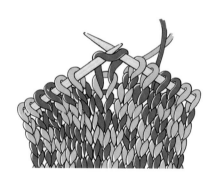

A chart is usually provided in the form of a grid with each square representing 1 stitch. Each square on the grid is coloured to show the yarn to be used for each stitch (see Reading charts).

When following the chart, yarn not being used is carried along the back of the work until it is needed again. This leaves a short length of yarn across the back of your work, and is called stranding, or stranded knitting.

It helps to keep the 2 balls of yarn separate while knitting, in order to prevent them from tangling. Keep 1 ball on your right and 1 ball on your left.

As you change colour, simply let the current colour hang down at the back of the work until needed again and pick up the new colour to work the next stitch. Try not to pull too tightly when changing colours as this can pucker the stitches and spoil your tension/gauge.

The main thing to remember with colourwork knitting is to always feed in the yarns from the same position. Hold one colour at the top and the other colour at the bottom, keeping the same position throughout.

The yarn that you hold at the bottom will always be the more dominant colour and will stand out more in your knitted pattern.

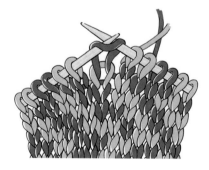

The yarn that you hold at the top will recede slightly.

When using stranded colourwork designs it may be worth playing around with yarn dominance on a small swatch, to see which you prefer. Or you can just hold your yarns in a consistent way throughout your project and not think about yarn dominance at all.

CASTING (BINDING) OFF

Knit cast (bind) off (in the round)

1. Knit 2 stitches (see Basic stitches – Knit stitch).

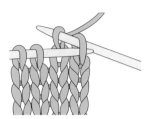 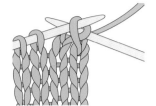 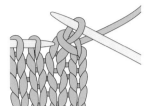 

2. Insert the tip of your left-hand needle into the first (bottom) stitch on the right-hand needle

3. Lift the bottom stitch over the top stitch and off the right-hand needle.

4. Knit another stitch so that you have 2 stitches on the needle again.

Repeat **Steps 3-4** until 1 stitch remains (if you are casting (binding) off all stitches).

5. Lengthen the last loop on your needle and cut working yarn.

6. Thread yarn tail onto tapestry/yarn needle and thread it from the back to front through the first cast (bind) off stitch.

7. Thread tapestry/yarn needle through the long loop and gently pull to join the stitches of the round.

8. Thread tapestry/yarn needle down through the centre of next cast (bind) off stitch and to the inside of your work and weave in tail.

Knit cast (bind) off (working flat)

To cast (bind) off a piece of knitting worked flat on 2 needles, work as for Knit cast (bind) off (in the round) until you have the last loop on your needle. Cut yarn and fasten off.

Three-needle cast (bind) off

This is a great technique to use when casting (binding) off 2 sets of live stitches together (as in the two-needle sock recipe (see Sock recipes), to join the toe seam).

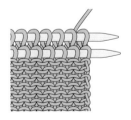 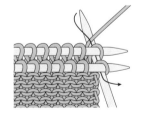 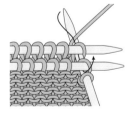 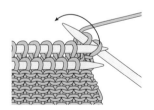

1. With right sides of work together and wrong side facing outwards, hold both needles in your left hand and line up the corresponding stitches. Make sure that your needles are both pointing the same way.

2. Using a third needle, insert needle into the first stitch on each of the 2 needles and knit the 2 stitches together with your working yarn. Slip them off the needle as you would a regular knit stitch.

3. Repeat **Step 2** to knit the next pair of stitches. You now have 2 stitches on the right-hand needle.

4. Using one of the left-hand needles, insert tip into the first (bottom) stitch on right-hand needle and lift it over the top stitch to cast (bind) off.

Repeat **Steps 3-4** until you've cast (bound) off all stitches.

Jeny's surprisingly stretchy cast (bind) off (by Jeny Staiman)

This is perfect for toe-up socks as the extra 'yarn round needle' provides elasticity and stretch. To maintain your rib pattern, work in your established rib pattern, taking yarn around needle in the same way to form a stitch, but making sure that you alternate correctly between your knit and purl stitches. This guide demonstrates with a 1 x 1 rib.

1. First, knit 1 st (the yarn is at the back of the work).

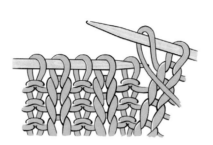

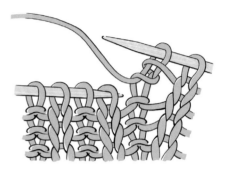

2. Bring yarn forward and all around needle and back to the front, to form a stitch (this is also called yarn over), then purl next stitch.

3. Insert the tip of your left-hand needle into the yarn over and also into the first (bottom) stitch on the right-hand needle. Lift the yarn over and bottom stitch over the top stitch and off the right-hand needle.

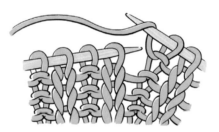

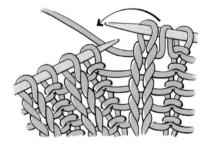

4. Yarn is at front after your previous purl stitch, take yarn to back between needles and then forward and over the right-hand needle and to the back of work again to form a stitch (this is also called a backward yarn over), then knit the next stitch.

5. Insert the tip of your left-hand needle into the yarn over and also into the first (bottom) stitch on the right-hand needle. Lift the yarn over and bottom stitch over the top stitch and off the right-hand needle. Yarn is at the back after previous knit stitch.

Repeat **Steps 2-5** until 1 stitch remains.

6. Lengthen the last loop on your needle and cut working yarn. Thread yarn tail onto tapestry/yarn needle and thread it from the back to front through the first cast (bind) off stitch (see Knit cast (bind) off (in the round)).

7. Thread tapestry/yarn needle through the long loop and gently pull to join the stitches of the round. Thread tapestry/yarn needle down through the centre of next cast (bind) off stitch and to the inside of your work and weave in end.

FINISHING YOUR PROJECT

Grafting/Kitchener stitch

1. To set up, hold the remaining sts on 2 DPNs parallel, with wrong sides of knitting facing each other and right sides facing outwards, and with the sts attached to the working yarn on the back needle. Cut the working yarn, leaving a long tail and thread onto a tapestry/yarn needle.

2. Insert tapestry/yarn needle into first st on front needle *purlwise*. Pull yarn through, leaving st on the needle.

3. Insert tapestry/yarn needle into first st on back needle *knitwise*. Pull yarn through, leaving st on the needle.

4. Insert the tapestry/yarn needle into the first st on the front needle *knitwise* and slip it off the end of the needle.

5. Insert the tapestry/yarn needle into the next st on the front needle *purlwise*. Pull yarn through and this time leave st on the needle.

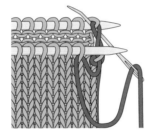 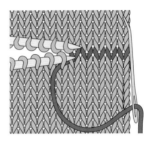

6. Insert the tapestry/yarn needle into the first st on the back needle *purlwise*, and slip it off the end of the needle.

Repeat **Steps 3-6** until all sts have been grafted together, stopping regularly to tighten up the stitches to create a tension/gauge that matches your knitting.

When you reach the end of your stitches, insert your tapestry/yarn needle down into the sock to the inside, through the middle of the next stitch on the main sock. Weave in end on wrong side.

Mattress stitch

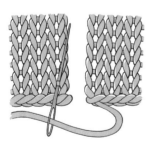 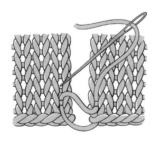

1. With right sides of both pieces of fabric towards you, secure yarn at the bottom of 1 piece. Pass needle to opposite section and insert needle though 1 stitch.

2. Pull yarn through and pull gently. Take needle to the opposite section and insert needle through 1 stitch of this section.

3. Continue in this way, from 1 side to the other as if lacing a corset, until you reach the last stitch.

4. Secure tightly. If you have entered through the right section as illustrated, the seam will be virtually indistinguishable from the rest of the fabric.

Always be sure to use the same colour of yarn as in the main body of work so that when the seams are pulled and moved when worn, the joining yarn cannot be seen. Some yarns may be too weak or fancy to sew along a seam, so double these up, add a stronger yarn to the original or use a different yarn, but ensure it is the same colour.

Weaving in ends

After finishing your project you will have several yarn ends to weave into your work from casting on, casting (binding) off, changing colours or adding in a new ball of yarn.

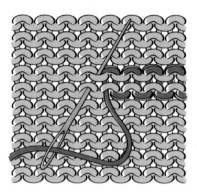

1. With wrong side of work facing, thread yarn end onto a tapestry/yarn needle and weave the yarn end in and out through the back of approximately 8 or 10 stitches along a row of stitches then turn and work back in the opposite direction.

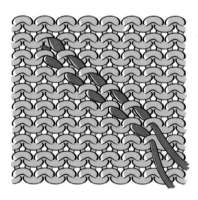

2. Alternatively, work diagonally up for a few rows, then back down to the original stitch, making sure nothing is visible from the right side. Where possible, weave ends into the seam stitches for approximately 8 to 10 stitches. Trim yarn end close to the work.

Fixing holes

If you find that you have small holes at the sides of heels where you may have picked up the extra heel stitches, you can fix these on the right side or the wrong side.

ON THE WRONG SIDE

1. Take a length of matching yarn and thread onto a tapestry/yarn needle. Turn your sock inside out so that wrong side is facing outwards.

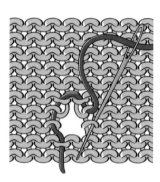

2. Weave your tapestry/yarn needle through the back bumps of the stitches around the hole, and gently pull the ends of your yarn to shorten the stitches and reduce the hole.

3. Tie off and weave in ends along the side of the heel to hide them.

ON THE RIGHT SIDE

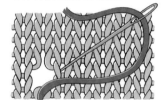

1. Thread matching yarn onto a tapestry/yarn needle, and with right side facing outwards, bring needle from inside of sock and through the base of the 'V' of a stitch.

2. Take needle through the legs of the stitch above (this is the same as working a duplicate stitch or Swiss darning) from right to left and back through the base of the stitch.

3. Pull gently on the ends of the yarn and tie off on the inside of the work, then weave in ends.

Blocking your project

Once you have finished your socks, it is recommended to block them, to help smooth out your tension/gauge and even out the stitches.

1. Fill a basin or bowl with cold or lukewarm water (check the ball band for temperature instructions). If desired you can add a small amount of detergent (such as a wool wash or a mild shampoo).

2. Place your socks into the water to wet them completely and leave them to soak for 10-15 minutes. Do not agitate them, otherwise you may cause them to felt and shrink.

3. Lift your socks carefully out of the basin or bowl and at the same time very gently squeeze out the excess water. Do not wring, otherwise you could damage your fabric. Also take care when lifting the socks out of the water when soaking wet, as your knitting may stretch.

4. Carefully lay your socks onto a dry towel then, starting at one end, loosely roll up the towel. Lightly apply pressure to squeeze out the excess water.

5. Unroll the towel then place your socks onto a blocking board with right side uppermost, and pin flat without stretching, using rust-proof pins or blocking pins. Alternatively you could place over sock blockers.

6. Leave to dry completely before removing the pins or before removing from sock blockers.

ABBREVIATIONS

B, add bead to next stitch using crochet hook, then knit this stitch

BC, background colour

C2Ftbl, place next stitch on cable needle, hold at front, k1tbl from left-hand needle, k1tbl from cable needle

cdd, slip next 2 stitches together knitwise, knit 1 stitch, pass 2 slipped stitches over the knitted stitch, to decrease 2 stitches

Cr8B, place next 5 stitches on cable needle, hold at back, k3 from left-hand needle, return 2 left-most sts from cable needle to left-hand needle, move cable needle to front, p2 from left-hand needle, k3 from cable needle

Cr8F, place next 3 stitches to first cable needle and hold at front, place next 2 stitches to second cable needle and hold at back, k3 from left-hand needle, p2 from back cable needle, k3 from front cable needle

DPN(s), double-pointed needle(s)

DS, double stitch (see Sock techniques: Short rows – Double stitch short rows)

k, knit

k2tog, knit 2 stitches together, to decrease 1 stitch

kfb, knit into the front and then the back of the next stitch, to increase 1 stitch

knitwise, insert needle as if to knit

M1L, make 1 stitch by picking up bar between current and next stitch from front to back onto left-hand needle, then knit this through the back leg

M1R, make 1 stitch by picking up bar between current and next stitch from back to front onto left-hand needle, then knit this through the front leg

MDS, make double stitch

p, purl

p2tog, purl 2 stitches together, to decrease 1 stitch

patt(s), pattern(s)

PC, pattern colour

pm, place marker

psso, pass slipped stitch over

purlwise, insert needle as if to purl

RS, right side

sk2po, slip 1, knit 2 together, pass slipped st over, to decrease 2 stitches

skpo, slip 1 stitch knitwise, knit 1 stitch, pass slipped stitch over the knitted stitch, to decrease 1 stitch

sl1, slip 1 stitch purlwise with yarn held in back unless otherwise indicated

sm, slip marker

ssk, slip next 2 stitches knitwise one at a time, knit these 2 stitches together through back leg, to decrease 1 stitch

st(s), stitch(es)

T2B, place next stitch on cable needle, hold at back, k1tbl from left-hand needle, p1 from cable needle

T2F, place next stitch on cable needle, hold at front, p1 from left-hand needle, k1tbl from cable needle

tbl, through the back leg

W&T, wrap and turn

WS, wrong side

wyib, with yarn in back

wyif, with yarn in front

yo, yarn over, to increase 1 stitch

ABOUT THE AUTHOR

Lynne Rowe is a knit and crochet designer, author and tech editor, and she loves to share her skills and techniques so that everyone can enjoy the benefits that knitting and crochet can bring, from relaxation and mindfulness, to creativity and a sense of achievement and pride.

Lynne has been crafting for most of her life and eventually turned her passion into a full-time career. You can follow her knit and crochet adventures on her website, or follow her on social media where she shares lots of free patterns, tips and advice:

Website: knitcrochetcreate.com

Instagram: @the_woolnest

Index

Allis, Anniken 124–7
arches 12–13

Balke, Kerstin 128–31
Barthold, Kaitlin 116–19
beading 124–7, 153
Becker, Judy 148
Bird, Vikki 100–3
blocking 34, 165
Brown, Abby 120–3

cable 28, 110, 147, 155
casting off 57, 161
casting on 44, 50, 52, 140–1, 146–9
charts, reading 150
colour 18–22
    changes 68, 158
    multi 20, 158–60
contrast elements 58–65, 66
crochet hooks 28, 34
cuff-down socks 42–9, 68
    contrast elements 66
    heels 78–81, 85
    projects 92–9, 104–7, 116–23, 128–31
    toes 88
    two at a time 140–2
cuffs 12–13, 70, 72–5
    contrast elements 66
    sock projects 92–4, 96–8, 100, 103–4, 107, 111–12, 115–16, 118, 120–2, 124, 127–8, 130
    sock recipes 45, 56, 60, 66
    types 74–5
cut-open tubes 34

decreasing 152–3

ends, weaving in 164

Fair Isle knitting 160
finishing 49, 57, 163–5
Fletcher, Rachel 104–7
foot 12–13
    circumference 14, 37, 40
    length 14, 15
    size 14–15, 37, 40
    sock projects 92, 95–6, 99–100, 102–4, 107–8, 111–12, 114, 116, 119–20, 124, 127–8, 130–1
    sock recipes 48, 54

garter stitch 78–80
grafting/Kitchener stitch 49, 92, 100, 108, 120, 163
gussets 12–13, 78–81, 84
    sock projects 92, 95–6, 99, 104, 107–8, 111–12, 114, 116, 119–20, 122–4, 127
    sock recipes 47–8, 64

heel flap 78–81, 84, 92, 95–6, 99, 104, 107–8, 111–12, 115–16, 118, 120, 122, 124, 127
heel turn 92, 96, 98, 104, 107–8, 111, 115–16, 118, 120, 122, 124, 127
heels 12–13, 70, 76–85, 100, 103
    common 78–9
    contrast elements 66
    double stitch short row (boomerang) 82, 128, 130
    forethought 85, 100, 103, 154
    garter stitch 80
    simple shaped 82
    slipstitch 80
    sock recipes 46–7, 54–5, 60, 62–3, 66
    striped (two-colour) 81
    toe-up 82–4
    wrap and turn short row 83
holes, fixing 164

increasing 151
insteps 12–13, 60–1

joining 44, 65, 135
Jorissen, Carmen 112–15

k3tog 152
kfb 151
kltbl 150
knit stitch 149
knitting in the round 132–43
    casting off 161
    joining 44, 135
    scrappy socks 68
    swatches 32, 34

lace 104–7, 118, 126
legs 12–13
    sock projects 94, 98, 100, 103–4, 107, 111–12, 115–16, 118, 120–2, 124, 127–8, 130
    sock recipes 45, 56, 60

magic loop knitting 26, 50, 53, 56, 136–8, 140–3
make 1 stitch 151
matching socks 22
materials 16, 18–25
mattress stitch 163

needles 26–7, 132–5
    cable 28
    double-pointed 26, 134–5
    flexible short 26, 138–9
    long-circular 26, 137
    short circular 26, 136
    tapestry/yarn 28
negative ease 15, 37, 40
no heel socks 68

P2tog 152
picking up stitches 154, 157
picot edge 75
Potter, Emma 96–9
pressure points 24
purl stitch 149

rib
    cable and twisted 110
    corrugated 75, 160
    half-twisted 75
rows, short 82, 156–7

'scrappy' socks 66, 68
seams 12–13, 65
shortie socks 68
side seams 65
sizing socks 14–15
sk2Po 153
slip stitch 80, 150
sock anatomy 12–13
sock elements 70–89
sock projects 90–31
    Autumn Berries 116–19
    Beads of Dew 124–7
    Bracken Cables 108–11
    Red Sky at Night 120–3
    Sloping Hills 92–5
    Spring Lace 104–7
    Summer Meadows 112–15
    Twisting Pathways 100–3
    Under the Stars 96–9
    Winter Snow 128–31
sock recipes 38–69
sock techniques 144–65
soles 12–13, 64
SSK 152

Staiman, Jeny 162
stitch directory 149–50
stitch holders 28
stitch markers 28
stocking stitch 78–9
stranded colourwork 160
stripes 22, 81
    jogless 159
superwash 24
swatches 32, 34–5

tension/gauge 27, 30–7, 40
toe-up socks 50–7, 68
    casting off 162
    contrast elements 66
    heels 82–4, 85
    projects 100–3, 112–15, 124–7
    toes 89
    two at a time 143
toes 12–13, 70, 86–9
    contrast elements 66
    sock projects 92, 95–6, 99–100, 102, 104, 107–8, 111–12, 114, 116, 119–20, 123–4, 127–8, 131
    sock recipes 48, 52–3, 61, 64–6
    types 88–9
tools 16, 26–8
two at a time knits 140–2

'vanilla socks' 40
Villareal, Olivia 108–11

Winwick Mum 92–5
wool 24, 32
wrap and turn 156–7

yarn 18–25, 28
    colour 18–22, 158–60
    fibres 24–5, 32
    matching 22
    meterage/yardage 32
    quantities 40
    substitution 32
    weight/thickness 25, 32
yarn over increases 151

THANKS

I love to share my knitting skills and knowledge, so it was such an honour to research and write this book all about sock knitting. It was a huge task to undertake and I couldn't have done it without the expert knowledge and support of my book editor Tricia and the wonderful team at David and Charles – to Sarah C for her encouragement and for believing in me; to Jeni, Sam and Sarah R for making every page look amazing; to Jason for his fantastic photography, and illustrators Cathy and Kang for their amazing artwork.

Enormous thanks to yarn dyer Kate Selene (www.kateselene.com) for kindly sending me the biggest bag of yarn oddments for knitting up samples and for winding into mini skeins for photography. Her colourful bag of possibilities made me so happy, and I can't wait to turn the rest into scrappy socks in every colour of the rainbow.

Thanks to all the amazing designers who created a wonderful collection of beautiful sock patterns, and to my friends Cassie and Christine who kept me going with their wise words of encouragement when I was flagging just a little. And where would I have been without the knitting support of Nicky, whose knitting is so beautiful and neat and perfect for close up photography.

Finally, I have my family to thank for putting up with my never-ending knitting exploits and those yarn deliveries that seem to occupy every nook and cranny of the house.

And last but not at all least, a huge thank you to everyone who has followed my design work or bought one of my books or attended one of my classes; your support is very much appreciated and I'm truly grateful.

Lynne xx

THE DESIGNERS

The author and publisher would like to thank all of the designers whose sock projects appear in this book.

ANNIKEN ALLIS
@yarnaddictanni

KERSTIN BALKE
@stine_und_stitch

KAITLIN BARTHOLD
@originally.lovely

VIKKI BIRD
@vikkibirddesigns

ABBY BROWN
@cozy_crafting

RACHEL FLETCHER
@twinsetandpurl

CARMEN JORISSEN
@newleafdesigns.nl

WINWICK MUM
@winwickmum

EMMA POTTER
@potterandbloom

OLIVIA VILLAREAL
@thishandmadelife

A DAVID AND CHARLES BOOK
© David and Charles, Ltd 2021

David and Charles is an imprint of David and Charles, Ltd
Suite A, Tourism House, Pynes Hill, Exeter, EX2 5WS

Text and Designs © Lynne Rowe 2021
Layout and Photography © David and Charles, Ltd 2021

First published in the UK and USA in 2021

Lynne Rowe has asserted her right to be identified as author of this work in accordance with the Copyright, Designs and Patents Act, 1988.

The author and publisher have made every effort to ensure that all the instructions in the book are accurate and safe, and therefore cannot accept liability for any resulting injury, damage or loss to persons or property, however it may arise.

Names of manufacturers and product ranges are provided for the information of readers, with no intention to infringe copyright or trademarks.

A catalogue record for this book is available from the British Library.

ISBN-13: 9781446308523 paperback
ISBN-13: 9781446380406 EPUB
ISBN-13: 9781446380390 PDF

This book has been printed on paper from approved suppliers and made from pulp from sustainable sources.

Printed in the UK by Pureprint for:
David and Charles, Ltd
Suite A, Tourism House, Pynes Hill, Exeter, EX2 5WS

10 9 8 7 6 5 4 3 2 1

Publishing Director: Ame Verso
Senior Commissioning Editor: Sarah Callard
Managing Editor: Jeni Chown
Project Editor: Tricia Gilbert
Head of Design: Sam Staddon
Design and Art Direction: Sarah Rowntree
Pre-press Designer: Ali Stark
Illustrations: Kuo Kang Chen and Cathy Brear
Photography: Jason Jenkins
Production Manager: Beverley Richardson

David and Charles publishes high-quality books on a wide range of subjects. For more information visit www.davidandcharles.com.

Share your makes with us on social media using #dandcbooks and follow us on Facebook and Instagram by searching for @dandcbooks.

Layout of the digital edition of this book may vary depending on reader hardware and display settings.